Boss Psychology

Help Your Boss Make You a Success

Boss Psychology: Help Your Boss Make You a Success

Charles C. Vance

McGraw-Hill Book Company

New York   St. Louis   San Francisco   Auckland   Düsseldorf
Johannesburg   Kuala Lumpur   London   Mexico   Montreal
New Delhi   Panama   Paris   São Paulo   Singapore
Sydney   Tokyo   Toronto

Library of Congress Cataloging in Publication Data

Vance, Charles C
  Boss psychology.

  1. Psychology, Industrial. 2. Supervisors.
I. Title.
HF5548.8.V27   158.7   74-23612
ISBN 0-07-066871-X

1234567890 BPBP 784321098765

*The editors for this book were Robert A. Rosenbaum and
Patricia A. Allen, the designer was Naomi Auerbach, the
production supervisor was Teresa F. Leaden. It was set in
Optima by Progressive Typographers.*

It was printed and bound by The Book Press.

Contents

people so hostile to business? Why does anyone want to be a boss? What do bosses want most? Understanding your boss's actions. Do you deal your boss four aces? Have some heart for the executive biggies. Cherries on top of the whipped cream. The day-after-day struggle on the job. What you owe yourself in the business world. Which way to look? A way out, a way up? What do you expect from your present job? Leave the office in a cheerful mood. Have you changed your "boss"-and-"bossed" concept?

3. *Your Role in Creating Better Bosses*

Bosses are the business world's main foundation. What the business world wants of its many bosses. What the future looks like for bosses. You can help your boss move up. You can play havoc with your boss's plans. How Old Frightful became a boss. How a nice person made it to bossdom. How another nice person launched a good career. The fashion of taking cheap shots at bosses. Ways to make your boss a more effective manager. What business trends mean to your chances. Results you can expect in making your boss a friend. Your boss isn't your enemy, your wrong emotions are.

4. *The New Ms. and Her Boss*

Farewell to the old office Miss and Mrs. The opening world of women's opportunities. The problems the Ms. has in meeting the business world. Advantages the new Ms. gives the business world. The new Ms. and her ability to manage others in business. Understanding the married woman worker in the group. Understanding the single young girl in the group. What any woman must remember about business. Why some bosses keep themselves aloof. Look for the friend in your very own boss. The touchiest point: what women are paid.

5. *Fitting Yourself Snugly into the Business World*

Contemplation over your breakfast coffee. Forming this day's game plan on your way to work. Smoothing out today's emotional highs and lows. Digging more for yourself out of this business day. Sidestep damaging situations today. What you can accomplish for yourself this day. Lunch time: ask yourself, "What do I believe about business?" The afternoon: stepping up your self-esteem. Setting up a successful business day tomorrow. Quitting time, and you're still in charge of your own destiny. That wonderful feeling of emotional balance. After work: what you owe your family and friends. You owe yourself a large measure of excellent health. The different roles you act out each day. Come on, admit it. You want to like yourself. You'll find courage to meet big changes. The tremendous power of common courtesy. These positive thoughts help you every work day.

to enjoy misery of your own making. Should you confide in your boss and the others? Never leave the office in an angry mood.

Preface

Are you, like many thousands of other people in the business world, missing one of the truly great opportunities both to protect your job and to make solid advancement toward goals that are extremely worthwhile to you?

It is the splendid opportunity to help your boss make you a success by using "boss psychology." It is an opportunity that exists regardless of whether your relationship with your boss is presently good, passable, or bad. It is a favorable chance for you to strengthen your hold on the job you now have and to break out of any restrictive situation in which you might be trapped. It is a proved method which opens the way for you to move energetically toward the rewarding kind of success you would like to have in the business world.

The concept of *using "boss psychology" in helping your boss make you a success* might at first be troublesome for you to accept. It may be that you've never viewed any boss as being anything but an authority figure, perhaps an obstacle, a glory seeker, or a miscarriage of justice. Like most people who work for a living, you may have stood too much in awe of the bosses you've had.

This book will show you some of the truths about bosses, *especially yours.* It will help correct your blindness to your boss as both a human being and someone who can help you if you in turn help this person. This blindness is not unusual in the business world. It has hampered the rise of many men and women who had fine potentials but failed to take advantage of boss psychology to protect their jobs and find the right path to success.

Bosses constitute one of the most misunderstood areas of the business world. Take *you,* for example. All your life you've been under the supervision of other people—parents, older brothers and sisters, relatives, teachers, camp counselors, summer job managers, professors, and bosses of every kind. In most cases you instinctively worked out some sort of compromise with these people that allowed them to govern you at times and allowed you some freedom to develop on your own.

Like the rest of us, you accepted the fact that *someone* inevitably has control over you for a portion of each day. In a few cases you've enjoyed being bossed because you felt you benefited and that the boss helped make it enjoyable. In other cases you went along passively. In some of these instances you gained nothing. You even found ways to subvert the boss, to counterattack, as it were, to resist, and to negate.

Are you ready now for this new concept of bosses? All you need to do is view your relationship with your boss in the light of what it can do for *your own best self-interest.* Ask yourself a few preliminary questions at this point:

1. Why am I dissatisfied with my job?

2. Am I being treated fairly?

3. How do I characterize my relationship with my boss: good, passable, or bad?

4. Is the relationship between my boss and me primarily a result of my boss's actions or of mine?

5. Has my boss made any serious effort to understand me and what I'd seriously like to get out of the business world?

6. Have I made any concentrated effort to understand my boss and what I can do to help the boss?

7. Why haven't I made the progress to which I feel I'm entitled?

8. Have I built a wall around myself to protect me from the business world and the people in it, particularly my boss?

9. Do I have a definite plan for where I want to go in the business world or am I "free-floating?"

10. Am I really listening to what my urgent sense of self-interest warns me I should be doing?

Be honest with yourself. Don't hedge or gloss over your emotions. You know *right now* whether you're happy or unhappy with your job, your boss, and your organization. Possibly you are in between, contented at times and unhappy at others. What makes you feel contented? What makes you unhappy?

Like a compass needle, you'll find your thoughts coming back to your boss. Your boss *is* an important key to your happiness or dissatisfaction. Your boss can be like a solid block of stone that holds nothing for you but tasteless dust if you halfheartedly try to chip through it. Or your boss can be a friend who can hasten your success and help you rise higher in the business world than you might now believe to be possible.

You had nothing to do with the selection of your boss. You have *everything* to do with establishing the proper kind of working relationship that *makes the boss a winner and you a winner.* One of the most fraudulent concepts about bosses is that if a subordinate helps a boss, only the boss wins. Misconceptions such as this can cost you *money* and time in going places in the business world.

There are hundreds of damaging misconceptions about bosses. Many of them were handed down over the centuries, fed by the emotions of people who served tyrannical or paternalistic bosses of other years—and fed, also, by those who served unhappily in the military, in government, and in hundreds of poorly organized businesses.

The true picture of a boss is not very clear in most people's minds. For one thing, no one really likes the idea of having a boss. No one cottons to the idea of having someone keeping an eye on them. No one wants to report to someone else. The system makes for potential abrasiveness that, unchecked, can constantly rub both the boss and the employee the wrong way.

That the boss system has lasted this long and has grown larger is a tribute to the stonelike fact that most people *do* need someone keeping an eye on them. This fact requires both the boss and the employee (that's you) to learn to live with this potential abrasiveness and to make mutual progress in spite of it. None of us work as hard for ourselves as we do for someone who has authority over us—not when a paycheck is involved.

No army would move, no organization would function, no business would prosper if there were no bosses whatsoever. Can you imagine what education, government, industry, science, the military, and other organizations would be like if there were no chain of command? Even the theater, art, literature, and motion pictures have disciplinarians, bosses of a kind, masters who make all beginners and practitioners "look up" to the bosses' achievements and constantly try to improve their efforts.

So it is with you.

You can win greater success with the help of your boss. You can gain promotions, advancements, benefits, better working conditions, greater security, and more satisfaction *and be more in control of your own destiny* by knowing the boss system, by knowing your boss, and by using boss psychology to help your boss make you a success.

"Boss psychology" is not a means of manipulating a boss in order to gain advantages for yourself. "Boss psychology" is the complete awareness you have in knowing that when you actively help your boss achieve the group's goals you help yourself. It's as simple as that.

Why work passively for your boss? Give your boss plenty of reasons to work for you! This book shows you how it is being done every day by others who have studied boss psychology and found they could make it produce the riches of success for them.

Charles C. Vance

1

Why You Love
or Hate Your Boss

At some stage in your business-world life you fall prey to doubt, misgiving, and disenchantment with your job and with the boss you have. You begin to realize there is a serious conflict within you, a conflict between your youthful expectations of what the business world would be and your slow realization of what it actually is. You feel a persistent sense of threat and a deep anxiety that something has gone wrong.

At this stage it is easy for you to try to blame the boss for what bothers you. You find it difficult to understand that the anxiety you feel is out of proportion to the reality of the situation. You are deeply troubled by what you feel is a severe lack of security.

It is at this point that *you* must come to understand *why* you love or hate your boss. You have, over the years, come to involve all of your bosses in your quest for security. This is normal; we all do it. What can be abnormal is the desperate *manner* in which you confuse your boss with your security.

Let's examine what the word "security" means to you. It is your human need to increase your feelings of esteem and respect for yourself. When you feel there is a serious threat to your self-esteem and self-respect, you become anxious, developing a sort of free-floating nervousness that pervades everything you do and think. You come under a strain and have a period of stress, a very uneasy time.

You respond to anxiety of this type by trying to find ways to relieve the stress. You look for someone to blame for this nameless threat to your security. Your boss is a highly visible target because the boss's approval or disapproval of you as a person or of your work performance as a subordinate is directly related to the good or bad way you feel about yourself.

You often don't realize that this approval or disapproval factor is tied into the aggregate level of approval or disapproval you have experienced from *everyone* who bossed you from early childhood. If you are dissatisfied with the progress you've been making, if you are uneasy about the business world, if you are unhappy with yourself, your problem is *you* and not your boss.

This chapter has a goal—to take you by the shoulders and shake you until you understand that it is not your boss who is causing problems, *it's you*. You aren't taking advantage of the opportunities your job and your boss hold for you. These opportunities, when you see them and grab them, will lead you to a string of higher salaries, more benefits, and more meaningful achievements.

It makes no difference whether you are young, mature, or a senior citizen, flirtatious or shy, strong or weak, bold or cowardly, tall or short, bald or hairy, plump or skinny, woman or man. The opportunities are there for you to increase your security, to reinforce your self-esteem and self-respect. You can do something *right now* that will do wonders for you.

You can, with a different outlook about your boss and about bosses in general, come to realize more of your full potentials as a person. You can gain greater achievements in your work that are in line with your purpose in life. The starting point is to understand *why* you love or hate your boss.

Don't kid yourself that you "feel nothing" about your boss. It doesn't work that way. You feel *something*—admiration or despisal, respect or disrespect, closeness or distance, rapport or coolness, affection or displeasure, approval or dislike. In one form or another you love or hate your boss. Let's examine the *why* of your love or hate for your boss by taking a closer look at what we mean by "boss" and at some of the things that make you tick in the business world.

A boss by any other name

"Boss"? The word certainly means different things to different people. The *Oxford Universal Dictionary* says an early use of it dates back to 1822 with the Dutch adjective "baas," which meant *master*.

In the United States, "boss" came to mean anyone who was a business manager or had the right to give orders. In England, workmen used "swell" or "top-sawyer" for the same meaning. By 1882 "boss" also had come to cover a manager or a dictator of a political organization.

To be a boss today is to be in control of other people and to manage their work. (It is not to be confused with Bailey's observation in 1657 that a boss was a "water conduit running out of a gor-bellied figure.")

In *Danny's Own Story*, by Donald Robert Perry Marquis, is the statement, "A man jest naturally got to have something to cuss around and boss, so's to keep himself from finding out he don't amount to nothing." Advice to the Class of 1929, Massachusetts Institute of Technology, by Robert Emmons Rogers, included "Marry the boss's daughter."

The word "manage" comes to us from the Latin "manus," *hand,* and the French "manège," which describes horsemanship, or riding control. Today it means to control the affairs of an organization, most generally a business organization, but there are also managers of athletic groups, choirs, musical groups, and so on. There's a manager for almost every United States group activity.

We're of two minds about using the word "boss" in this country. Few people say, "Good morning, *boss*." A secretary, for example, will refer to "Mr. Jones" when talking about the boss at the office. A manager in a meeting will say, "This is what the vice president wants." Others will refer to "Al" or "Pete" or "Mary" or "J. C."

Nearly all of them, on the other hand, will say, "Wait 'til I tell you the stupid thing *my boss* did today," when they're in the safe zone of their families or with close friends. This split personality in the use of the word "boss" explains some of our present-day difficulties in the business world. At work we like to pretend that we're nearly equal to our superior, that, indeed, the boss is not a "superior" but merely a person who happens to be in charge of our work. We feel we don't really need a boss. A boss is just there because the organizational chart calls for someone to be there. At home or away from the office we drop this silly pretense and admit that we are governed almost totally by a boss.

Did you see yourself in the paragraphs above? Did you ask yourself how much you are involved in this game of split personality? My guess is that you're like the rest of us. You've been following a pattern set decades ago when the movement for greater personal freedom "on the job" began to take root and grow.

Why some people want to change the boss system

The recent growth of freedom on the job has been phenomenal when compared with the sweatshops of the turn of the century, the paternalistic manufacturing companies prior to World War

II, and the older plantation-type enterprises that held many workers in virtual bondage and required them to accept scrip for their work and to trade solely at the company store.

The growth of freedom on the job is still hampered by the split personality we possess in relation to our bosses. Few of us are brave enough to say, "I don't want any boss at all. I want to be left on my own to do my work uninhibited and unfettered by the whims, moods, and prejudices of a superior." We still allow the authority figure of the boss to control and influence us.

Many American youths, unhappy with what happened to their parents in the business world, have elected to work elsewhere under different conditions. They closed the door against bosses, but they closed the door to themselves as well. They can't use the business world to advance themselves. The sad truth is that, no matter where they went, there was some form of boss for them to deal with. Still, they avoided being gobbled up by business and becoming persons who docilely accept a master at the office but who complain bitterly at home about "the system."

While we're on the subject of words, notice that we still use "subordinate" and "superior." How painfully definite are these two words. The first is clearly inferior to the second, the second is clearly dominant to the first. As a "superior" a man or woman says, "I am the boss!" The hidden meaning is: "I am better than the others. They are working for *me*."

As a "subordinate" we rebel against the word. We say, "He's not a boss, he's an obstacle." We don't believe in the "boss system" unless *we* become a boss of someone. Then it is a different matter. Until then we say, "I don't regard myself as being inferior or subordinate to anyone."

In the pyramid structure of the business world, hedging about words and definitions is useless against the cold organizational charts that state that some few people are bosses and many are bossed. So the emotional conflict goes on between what is and what we would like it to be.

Will the "boss system" ever change? It has changed and it will continue to do so. Slowly. Perhaps so painfully slowly that you won't notice too much dramatic change in the decade ahead. Bosses have been around for a long time, but the American people are pushing vigorously for changes in the *ways* in which they are bossed.

These changes include having more to say about the decision-making process, about who become bosses, about how they conduct the office, and about the rights of the individual who is bossed. Not many managements operate in a free, democratic manner, but there are forces at work to *make* them become more democratic, more responsive to the people's needs. The civil rights movement has pried loose more jobs for blacks and other minority groups. Women have earned more management titles and responsibilities and have taken many jobs formerly held by men. Yes, changes are taking place before our eyes.

The business structure and the boss concept

The business structure is firmly based on the boss concept. Theoretically, bosses have subordinates to help make decisions and carry out the work flow efficiently and profitably. In practice, many bosses still allow their personal whims, biases, and prejudices to be the sole basis for many of their decisions. It is hard to root out *that* factor.

I mentioned the youths who abhor the American business system. I'll mention some other signs, obvious to you as well as to me, of a growing independence of Americans from the system.

1. The growth of small businesses where a person can avoid having a boss—where individuals can win or lose on their own efforts.

2. The rapidly escalating "early retirement" movement by

men and women who want to get out of business as fast as they can. Many are going into work which pleases them more, even if they make far less money. Others simply want to enjoy the remaining years of their life on whatever pension or profit-sharing money they have coming to them.

3. The number of university graduates who are going into public service rather than getting lost in the tangled trails of business.

4. The number of business organizations which have been forced to adopt some form of "job enrichment," "continuing education," or "personal development programs" to satisfy the demands of their employees.

5. The rising tide of articles in the daily newspapers and periodicals which place spotlights on the dark alleys of the American free enterprise system to the blinking dismay of many old-line executives. There is also a growing number of excellent articles for employees to show them how they can adjust to the inconsistencies and frustrations of working for a living.

There is no massive, unified campaign to change the "boss system." Those of us who toil for our paychecks are boxed within this structure for the foreseeable future. We must make the most of it to better ourselves and to gain for ourselves and our families as many of the good things as we can.

The "boss system" can be made to work for you. You can become a boss yourself—a finer one than those who bossed you on the way up. You have many advantages today that perhaps they did not have.

The business world may be criticized, scorned, publicly flagellated, mocked, satirized, spat upon, decried, and viewed with alarm. But it exists, and it is strong-walled and nearly impossible to bring tumbling down. Like all vast areas of human endeavor, it has its finer features. One of those features is the opportunity for you to achieve finer things for yourself.

The business structure has its walls and ramparts, but it also has drawbridges and gates which allow enterprising and ambi-

tious persons such as you to enter and to win and enjoy the
security and pleasures which you deserve.

What major force makes
your boss move?

Let's put some labels on the forces behind many bosses.

1. "Please like me and accept me." This boss deeply wants
to be liked and accepted by those in the group. You'll find this
boss in many of the lower echelons of business. Warm-hearted
and personable, this boss often lacks the drive and competitiveness to rise higher.

2. "I'm a professional and I get things done." This boss is out
to do things, to rack up a lot of impressive achievements. What
this boss loves is the thrill of reaching objectives and going on
to bigger and more tricky ones.

3. "I'm the boss and what I say goes." The business world
seems to be full of this power-driven, often unscrupulous type
of boss. Basically, a boss of this type is extremely insecure. The
protection this boss seeks is virtually total power over you and
the others in your group through intimidation rather than persuasion.

Can you figure out what force motivates *your* boss? To be
liked by everyone, to build a little empire, or to be all-powerful?
Do some thinking about it. Your boss will give you plenty of
clues about the motivation aspect. Some bosses have the good
elements of all three forces behind them. When they do, they
frequently develop into effective managers and are on their way
to becoming good executives.

Which label do you put on your boss?

The teeter-totter affair
between you and your boss

You are wise enough to know that you can either get too close
to your boss or get too far away from him. Some people have

affairs with their bosses that constantly teeter-totter—warm one day, cold the next. The ideal situation for *you* is a level affair where you each have confidence in the other and where there are very little if any up-and-down, warm-and-cold aspects to your relationship.

Fine. How do you manage this? First, by avoidance. You want to avoid too much dependency on your boss which can be very troublesome for you if the boss shifts weight and you're precipitously dipped into the unwelcome cold of being "out." Second, you want to achieve a harmonious working relationship in which your boss *does not* place a top-heavy dependency on you—in short, where the boss does not grandly and blindly expect you to be a worker of miracles, rescuing assignments headed for sheer failure in the hands of others.

Third, you can't take your association with your boss for granted. It requires care and feeding each working day—a delicate touch, you might say, to keep things from swinging either way. This is the total-awareness factor. When you *are* sharply aware of the critical nuances of human relations, you come to see that all effective associations with other people are based on solid trust between you and them. The relationship is more demanding between you and your boss because you want to mine some success from your boss. In a similar manner, your boss is using you to get more success out of the business world as well.

When you have these facts firmly in mind, you will be truly sensitive to your need to maintain a level affair with your boss. In such knowledge there is great power for you.

What's waiting for you down the business road?

"If I had it to do all over, I'd have worked for a half-dozen companies," a financial executive of a large company told me. "I would have enjoyed life a lot more." Nearing sixty, he had been with the same company for thirty-five years, his only job after graduating from college.

"I made a terrible mistake by moving from one company to another," a woman executive told me. "I should have settled down at the start and stayed with one good company. Today I'd have the protection of a retirement plan." She hedged from telling me her age, but from her gray hair and a knowledge of her career I guessed she was in her middle fifties. Extremely talented, well accepted, she had done very well in the business world. She, like the financial executive above, was corrosively unhappy.

One stayed, one moved around, and to them both the taste of success had become bitter. Despite their recognized success, they both had feelings of futility. When you talk to people who have "made it," you'll often find similar feelings that "something went wrong." These successful people feel they made deadly mistakes in setting out on their travels in the business world.

The feeling is common to us all. It will come to you unless you understand what is waiting for you in the business world and what you can do within your field of endeavor to make it truly meaningful for you. That which you may regard as a promising route to the top of the heap may end up being a dead-end street empty of satisfaction and of the wonderful sense of achievement that brings true happiness along with it. How can you avoid this type of disillusionment? You remind yourself of these important facts:

1. You can't trust blindly to luck that you will end up both a success and happy with your lot in life.

2. You must be adaptable in moving from job to job in or out of your company until you find a definite course that will take you to where you will be more satisfied.

3. Finding this course is never easy, and the biggest motivation for you are sudden crises which force you to decide

whether to stay where you are, hold to the course you are on, or look for better opportunities elsewhere.

4. These crises can be of any shape or nature: your boss leaves, your company is acquired by another, your job is changed severely, or top management shifts course and moves into areas not attractive to you. You are forced to reevaluate your position and make a decision.

5. Your reevaluation is based on what you *expected* out of the business world and what you have *gained* at this point. Often your dreams have not been fulfilled and you find yourself frustrated, unhappy, and adrift.

6. You confront yourself. Have you partially adapted to the changes you've experienced? Do you still want to fight for your dreams? Are you flexible enough to either change your dreams for something less attractive or change your occupation and continue your serious quest for a meaningful life?

What's waiting for you is what you're willing to settle for.

Sit behind yourself
for a change of view

Every carnival has a hall of mirrors where you see yourself from the side and behind. You need to see yourself from other viewpoints, as your boss sees you. The business world has a lot of people in it who have never been through a personal hall of mirrors.

Here are some examples:

1. The guy who arrives at his desk long before everyone else and who is the last to leave at quitting time.

a. He sees himself as setting a great example of a conscientious worker who by dint of long perseverance deserves to go someplace.

b. His boss and coworkers see him as a colorless drudge who could do his work in normal time but who spreads it out to make it appear as if he is working harder than anyone else.

2. The girl who wears miniskirts or tight knits and who swirls around in activity resembling that of an actress in a stage play.

a. She sees herself as deliciously imparting some drama and excitement to the office, pepping up the place, drawing admiring glances from the men and envious looks from the other women.

b. The men like the show of legs and other things, but they avoid getting too close to her because she comes on too strong. Being seen at the water cooler with her would start the gossip tongues going. The women look at her, not with envy, but with disgust. She should hear what they say about her in the restroom!

3. The bosses who pack an attaché case full of work to take home and like to be *seen* packing it.

a. They see themselves as carrying a terrible burden of responsibility and think that only they can move ahead because they give so much to the company by taking work home. They fancy themselves as dedicated and deliberately save work to be done at night because they "can't get things done at the office with all the interruptions."

b. The people under them think they are showoffs. Most of them think such bosses are nuts. Their family agrees because they work at night and on weekends, or they fall asleep after dinner and are about as much fun as sleeping bears. Their loved ones are losing interest in them.

What about you? Have you made a serious effort to see yourself as others see you? There is one guiding rule you can almost always depend on: *no one really sees you as you see yourself.* Your view of yourself is based largely on emotions. You act things out as everyone else does, nearly always unconsciously, through habits acquired and strengthened over the years, through picking up bits and pieces of character from others along the way of life and from experience.

People's opinion of you comes from what they see you do,

from how you look and how you express yourself. If you feel insecure and full of anxiety, they may see you as strong, dependable, and likeable. If you feel very special, a bit unusual, a step above everyone else, they may see you as a poser, a grandstander, a shallow person, someone who is inconsiderate and not very captivating.

If you feel homely and not exactly an exciting movie star, and though you are depressed by your lack of beauty or handsomeness, they may see you as a very special person who doesn't put on airs, who is fun to be with, and who is fully acceptable. If you feel that because you lack a university education you aren't very bright in comparison with those who have a college degree or two, the others may see you as a hardworking person who has native talent and who is far preferable to those who flaunt their degrees.

Try sitting in back of yourself once in a while. It's a terrific experience when you get it to work.

Can you put a true dimension to yourself?

You, like the rest of us, are troubled by some difficult questions. Who are you? Where did you come from? Where are you going? What makes you tick? What do you want out of life? What do you want from yourself? What mark do you want to leave in the business world?

"It's impossible for you to know yourself to the absolute fullest extent," an association president told me. "You'll keep surprising yourself by some of the things you say, do, and think. You'll change from time to time and never be certain how much or why."

You are one of the mysteries of the universe. Who were your ancestors of thousands of years ago? What did you inherit from them? What did your parents and your childhood environment do to fashion you the way you are today? What accumulated effect have your experiences had on you?

Difficult questions! If you knew the correct answers, you could put an accurate dimension to yourself. You must do what the intellectuals and prophets have pointed out for centuries. You must take yourself as you are right now and do the best, the very best, with what you have in intelligence, talent, determination, and desire. It is your challenge, and no one else's responsibility, to make yourself as complete a person as you can and to win as much as you can from your work on the job.

You must make the effort every day to:
- Reduce the illusions you have about yourself.
- Eliminate the illusions you have about the business world.
- Eliminate hostilities toward your boss and other people.
- Learn your limitations, so that you don't shoot too far over your head for the unattainable.
- Learn your strengths, so that you use them to gain more of the things you want out of life.
- Make yourself as attractive and as interesting to other people as possible within your capabilities.
- Love those who are closest to you and say so.
- Earn the love of those who mean the most to you.

The truth is that you can achieve far more in life than you think you can. The truth is that no one holds you back as much as you hold yourself back. The truth is that you can be far happier than you ever believed by *trying* to be happy and by *doing* those things that give you happiness from achievement.

The truth is that you are alone in this universe, locked into your mind and body, capable of enormous energy and great achievement—all by yourself—without anyone doing things for you or making the way easier.

In a quiet moment, take a piece of paper and put down your thoughts about yourself. Who are you? What do you want out of life? Why? Answer these troublesome questions as honestly as you can.

In your own way you'll put something of a dimension to yourself. "Know thyself" is an old biblical statement used in countless Sunday sermons. Know yourself, and you have moved closer to becoming a complete person.

Why did you choose the work you're in?

Here's a toughie. *Why* did you choose the line of work you are in?

_____I always wanted to be in this type of work.

_____It was my second choice, really; I actually wanted to be something else.

_____I more or less wandered into it—I didn't know what else I wanted to do.

_____I didn't think I was qualified to be anything else.

_____My parents insisted on it.

_____I was talked into it by a recruiter.

_____My family was in it, so I just picked it up.

_____A friend recommended me for an opening here.

_____I selected it because I felt I could make the most money at it.

_____I answered an ad in a newspaper.

Your answer reveals a lot. A great many people take the easy route of setting their sights very low and settling for less out of life. These people either lack education which would help them rise in the business world or they lack the initiative and drive to overcome lack of education, family support, and training. In other words, they don't try very hard. Education can be gained at any age. Initiative and drive can be turned on at any moment if a person decides to turn them on.

You chose the line of work you're in. No one *forced* you to accept it. And if you don't like it now, you can get out of it and into something that holds more excitement and challenge and the promise of success for you.

You are in charge of your life. If you hide behind some flimsy excuse as to why you continue to work at a certain job, you honestly can't blame anyone else for what happens to you. If you are in the exact line of work that you want to be in, if you enjoy it, if you take it as it is and try to improve your job and yourself at the same time, then you will win. You will win on your own, since you *are* in charge of yourself.

Your answer to the question of why you chose your line of work shows clearly whether *you've decided to be a winner or a loser.*

Now, about that love or hate thing

We've taken a look at you and a number of the things that reveal what sort of a person you are. Let's relate those things to your boss and try to discover how and why you react emotionally to the person to whom you report.

One of the finest human conditions attainable is when you feel a form of love for your boss. It means, basically, that you both have respect for each other. You find things about each other to approve. You find that when you're together there is a sort of electric crackle of enthusiasm and energy in the air. You're able to spark each other in your problem-solving efforts.

Love for your boss develops when you discover that you trust the boss and that you, in turn, are trusted by the boss. Trust is one of the great human emotions. It involves dignity, respect, admiration, and maturity.

When you feel a form of love for your boss, and when love is returned, your work days are pleasant, challenging, and rewarding. You enjoy going to work. You know there will always be problems, but you feel that with the boss's help you can overcome those problems. This solid working relationship allows you both to grow as individuals and to work harmoniously with each other to achieve the important objectives.

Unfortunately, the business world seems eternally bent on pushing people away from each other rather than on pulling them together. That's why most of us must cope with the unsettling conditions caused by a form of hate we feel for a boss. We must battle our wayward emotions in a constant effort to eliminate hate and to establish love.

I say *constant effort* because bosses change and you change. You may have a boss for whom you feel a form of love today. A week or a month from now, you may have a new boss, and the process of trying to establish that sense of trust begins all over again. It is a rare person who goes through a business career with one boss. It is even more rare for that boss to happen to be one who richly deserves the form of love we call "trust."

Love and hate can show up in odd ways. Love and hate both have myriad shadings and colorings. It seldom occurs to us to admit that we love or hate anyone, in those terms—let alone our boss. But in some form of emotional shading or coloring we do love or hate that person to whom we are so closely bound at the office or the plant.

Let's see what you get out of the following examples of people who failed to realize how their love or hate for their bosses affected them.

How Helen's emotions ruined her mornings

Helen was fresh from another battle with the commuter bus line. Nearly every day she had a quarrel with the driver or one of the passengers over virtually nothing. A short delay in the bus's arrival would set her off. A sudden nudge from another passenger would irritate her and she'd express her sentiments sharply. Her mornings were a mess, filled with hostility. Usually it was lunch time before she settled down.

She wrote letters to the president of the commuter line. She wrote letters to the editor of the newspaper, listing all the things she had to put up with while going to work.

It never occurred to her to wonder why when she was going

home she never picked quarrels with anyone. She sat peacefully reading the afternoon newspaper or looking out the window.

One morning she came apart over a small matter and threatened to sue the bus line. Her lawyer listened to her and said, "Who are you *really* mad at?" He had sensed what her problem was. "You seem to be using the bus line as a whipping boy."

Helen, with this start, eventually came to understand that what was upsetting her was not the bus service, but going to work and facing her boss every day. She had buried her dislike for him and transferred it to her *means* of getting to the unpleasant office situation. She requested a transfer and got it, along with a more pleasant boss, and began to live a more balanced life.

Are you doing Helen's act? Think about it. If you are, get your hidden emotions out in the open where you can examine them. Don't transfer them to others.

How Carl's emotions sent him on his way

Carl dreaded meeting his new boss. The old one had been a business-world abortion, nit-picky, abusive, demanding, intolerant. Carl had gotten nowhere with that boss, now moved to another division. Carl decided that the new boss would probably be as bad.

The new boss turned out to be totally different. He delegated authority smoothly and effectively. He spent time listening to Carl and the others in the group. He held short meetings that produced results. He encouraged Carl in all of Carl's assignments, made his approval clear when things went well, and didn't pop his cork when things got off the track.

Carl found himself buying new clothes without realizing that he wanted to appear more presentable at the office. He discovered the old fun of digging into his work. He found he could go to the boss with ideas and suggestions and not get a fish-eye look. Carl took some night courses to help him get on top of some new areas with which he wasn't familiar.

Each morning he went to work eagerly, feeling that he could accomplish things. The atmosphere of the group had improved so visibly that he was deeply affected by it. His own work was far more successful than it had been under the old boss.

Carl didn't know it, but the new boss had made a lover out of him instead of a hater. You saw it coming. When a promotion came along, Carl got it.

What would you expect from these four bosses?

Do you see your boss in this list of four basic types?

1. The skilled manager who by training and experience calmly goes about the task of running your group to win as many of its objectives as is possible.

2. The bootstrap manager, perhaps with only a high school education as a base, who has made it well up the ladder by sheer hard work and intense dedication. The bootstrap boss usually lacks the polish and poise of the skilled manager. What's worse, this boss tends to be extremely domineering and hard-nosed, hates competition, and strives to be all-powerful over the group.

3. The boss who occupies a position because of a family connection. It was easy for this boss to become a boss; the family power simply was such that room was made, needed or not. This boss may be very good, but most often this boss can be bad news because there is always the protective armor of the family.

4. The boss for which there is no clear explanation. This boss either outlived everyone else or obtained the position by a fluke of administration or at a time when there was no one else better qualified and when no effort was made to bring in or promote someone else.

Knowing which kind your boss is arms you with a better understanding of the person with whom you are dealing. More importantly, it arms you with knowledge of how much you can expect to gain from your relationship.

Remember that all bosses are mortals

By the time many bosses have reached the middle and upper echelons of management, they have acquired a certain air of authority. Authority tends to build a wall between those who have it and those who do not. This distance, in turn, tends to create the illusion that bosses can be a step above mortal emotions.

Don't you believe it. Any boss came from where *you* came from—the vast stockpile of raw human material—and is fully equipped with the same emotions that you have. The difference, coming from years of assuming authority over others, is in a boss's ability to *discipline* certain emotions.

Bosses may be able to discipline their anger, their frustration, their distaste, and their biases, but not always fully and forever. Every boss will erupt in a temper tantrum under certain conditions. Every boss will come near to going off the deep end at times. Every boss will come to the moment of saying, "It just isn't worth the money!"

If you are one of those who feel that a boss is "someone special," who is above human emotions, forget it. Bosses are mortals, just like you and me.

What do you fear most about facing your boss?

Which of these activities do you regard as the "most difficult" in regard to your personal confrontation with your boss?

1. Explaining where you unavoidably have made a mistake.
2. Avoiding being disagreeable about something the boss

has said or done when in truth you want to quarrel with it.

3. Refusing an assignment when you know it is over your head.

4. Challenging the boss on a point where experience has shown you the boss can't be changed

5. Playing office politics to win a promotion.

6. Telling the boss you're not getting fair credit for the work you've been doing.

7. Interrupting a meeting the boss is in to relay what you feel is an important bit of news.

8. Explaining how someone else made a costly mistake.

9. Pointing out that the boss's decision was a wrong one.

10. Telling the boss why you dislike someone in the group.

All of us hesitate to bring the boss bad news or to bring up an unpleasant subject. Bad news and unpleasant subjects are part of the business world. Difficult as these activities are, you must face them and get the task done. Tact and diplomacy are important ingredients of the manner in which you must handle such face-to-face discussions. Certainly you'll be worried. *That's normal.* But do them. *That's responsibility.*

Love or hate the boss, a way up or a way down

A good boss will make you feel significant, worthy, respected, and more in control of your own destiny. A bad boss will make you feel insignificant, unworthy, anxious, and blocked in your efforts to have something to say about who you are, where you're going, and how you'll get there.

The difference is that between having some trust, affection, and respect for your boss (which is earned) and some deep dislike and hostility which you feel for the boss because of the way the boss treats you. The fact that many people never understand fully how their bosses affect them doesn't change the situation.

Your boss has an impact on you—a deeper impact than you realize. The impact can boost you up the ladder because of the excellent motivations the love aspect has on you or it can plummet you downward because of the acidlike emotions with which the hate aspect subtly erodes you. It is up to you at this point to closely examine *how* you feel about your boss and *why*. You must be aware of the hidden emotions your boss evokes in you and the consequences of those emotions.

You love your boss if the boss has your self-interest in mind. You hate your boss if that person's actions and words show you that you don't count for much. There is no middle ground.

Some bosses are good to you because you are good to them. They repay a form of love with another form of love. Other bosses sense your dislike of them and find ways to repay it. They have emotions, too, and they react to the pressures of how they feel you regard *them*. It isn't a one-way street. You may be doing the right things that create harmony between yourself and your boss or you may be doing the wrong things that force you apart.

It's a tangled web, one that is difficult to sort out. Your task right now is to *think* about your relationship with your boss, to determine what you are doing and what the boss is doing. Don't throw up your hands and quit trying to figure it out. Your success in the business world is directly tied to your efforts to establish good working relations with your boss, good or bad, loved or hated.

The "why" you love or hate your boss is buried in all your actions, in all your expectations and those of your boss. Discover this hidden "why" and you have found the key to making your boss your friend.

Turning your boss into a friend isn't a cheap phrase. It has been done by countless others. *It can be done by you*. It starts with understanding *why* you feel about your boss the way you do.

Get busy working on this puzzle *right now*.

2

Changing the Snagging Concept of "Boss" and "Bossed"

On his thirty-fifth birthday Fred told his wife, "I'm never going to get anywhere." They were having dinner at a quiet downtown place. "Not with this company. My boss just isn't the kind of a guy I want to work for." He paused over the food he'd barely touched. "I've thought it all out. I guess I'll have to start looking around."

Fred had *not* thought it all out. His concept of a boss was the familiar one: the boss had all the power and Fred had none. In his view, Fred was powerless to deal with his boss. He accepted the "power" and did nothing to promote himself with his boss and to work out a better mutual arrangement that would allow him to advance in the company. Fred meekly had accepted being "bossed" as if he were a plantation slave and had no rights. He felt that his only out was to flee to another company, unaware that his snagging concept of "boss" and "bossed" would go right along with him.

Fred is far from being unusual. The notion that a boss *controls* a person, without any recourse or right of appeal, is nonsense, but it prevails everywhere. Take Barbara for another example.

Barbara worked in the payroll department of an insurance company. Her boss was an unmarried woman in her fifties who let everyone know how long she had done the same work that men did but for far less money. She was testy, domineering, and difficult to approach.

Barbara tried to present ideas and suggestions and was rebuffed time after time. After a while she quit trying. Her friends attempted to point out that she could have a showdown with her boss, that she could go over the boss's head to the manager of the division, that she could quit and get a better job somewhere else. Barbara's answer was, "There's nothing I can do." She sank into the role of a dull clerk, victimized, doing monotonous work, at the mercy of her unfeeling boss.

Here are the other sides of these two examples. Fred's boss regarded Fred as a softie, an employee who never spoke up, who went around the office with a long face, who gave no indication that he supported the boss or that he was eager to move ahead. Fred's boss had come to view him as just another inert body. He would have welcomed some energetic challenge from Fred, but none came, and Fred was virtually a forgotten person.

Barbara's boss was afraid of her. After struggling to gain a good position in competition with men, Barbara's boss feared she might lose her job to the younger, prettier, more innovative Barbara. It was fear that prompted this boss to behave in a distant, almost cruel manner to anyone she thought might try to take her job away from her. What Barbara didn't know was that the manager of the division was seeking someone to replace the boss, whose abrasiveness was well known.

By giving in to the wrong concept of "boss" and "bossed," both Fred and Barbara had literally cut to shreds their own opportunities for advancement. Let's explore more facets of this damaging concept which plagues so many people in the business world. It is a concept that has dulled many a promising person. It is a concept that is totally out of date, senseless, self-defeating, outrageous, and, to viewers of the business scene, nauseating.

We're going to show you that *you* need not become a victim of it.

We pay for what we accept

Too many of us accept the business world the way we find it. We lack the courage to challenge it and to try to change it. We pay for this lack of courage. We pay because we suffer under its rules when we played no role in forming those rules. We submit meekly, and sometimes the emotional price we pay is enormous in relation to what we get out of the business world.

We must work if we want to eat, own homes and cars, take vacations, and enjoy some of the good things of life. No one contests that fact. But who makes the rules under which we work?

There are plenty of rules to keep us working under the system. What rules are there to protect us and to allow us to have a hand in freshening and updating the system? We need more clear thinking and plain talking about the business world and about bosses in particular.

Let's put a spotlight on the business world first.

The business world is harshly criticized

Broad generalizations are lots of fun but meaningless. The business world has had many detractors and relatively few champions. It has been harangued, maligned, impugned, viewed with hositility, held in deep disrespect, treated with contempt, and attacked with viciousness. All of which, in one way or another, it has richly deserved.

An editor in Washington, D.C., gave me these broad "antibusiness" generalizations which he has heard most frequently:

1. Businesses manipulate in government to gain scandalous favoritism in regard to pricing freedom, regulation, and relief from prosecution.

2. Businesses deal with corruptible politicians to either gain laws that help them or prevent "harmful laws" from being passed.

3. Businesses pollute the water and air, by dumping chemicals, sludge, and effluent messes into our rivers, streams, and lakes and by allowing their smokestacks to carry noxious and dangerous pollutants into the air over our homes and schools.

4. Businesses destroy our environment, callously disregarding the ecological balance of nature, slashing down timberlands, or leaving ugly cesspools on our land.

5. Businesses are solely profit-oriented and stoop to any nefarious endeavor as long as it achieves the "bottom line" of hungry profit-making.

6. Businesses crow about actions "beneficial to society," but these are designed merely to camouflage their hidden efforts to influence greater profits.

7. Businesses shove off onto the public shoddy products that are unsafe and costly and that have early obsolescence deliberately built into them in order to gain greater profits.

8. Businesses dehumanize employees by giving them no voice in management decision-making, impose impersonal work methods, and rule with "you can be replaced" attitudes.

9. Businesses create within their ranks executives who are totally profit-oriented, care little about others, enrich themselves, and entrench themselves against any removal except that of death.

10. Businesses create a "dog eat dog" climate in which

young employees are encouraged *by example* to compete hotly against each other for promotions and become insensitive to anything but their own selfish interests.

11. Businesses "get away with murder" by circumventing and ignoring safety practices and laws as a way of making more money.

12. Businesses do not pay their shareholders fair and honest dividends; instead, they squander this money on huge salaries, plush comforts, and ill-planned ventures.

13. Businesses publish misleading and deliberately confusing financial statements.

14. Businesses say one thing publicly and do the opposite privately, such as running TV ads proclaiming they are working hard to prevent pollution while at the same time their lawyers are delaying the efforts of pollution-control agencies to enforce the laws.

You'll recognize these as only a few of the serious-minded charges against the American business establishment. You're familiar with them because they've been repeated in many forms in the news media for many years. They're all true. *Some* businesses somewhere are guilty of one or more of these actions. But certainly not *all* businesses are guilty.

Here's the balanced truth about businesses

Any careful student of the business scene knows that companies are run by men and women who, when they have an opportunity to enhance, better, and enrich themselves, will certainly do so. Each company seeks an advantage over its competitors. When executives feel they can gain a competitive edge in the marketplace, even for a short time, they will certainly do so.

Each company seeks assurance that it can stay in business for a long time and make money. If this involves dealing with politicians to get favorable government and judicial treatment, the executives will certainly consider doing and paying what is necessary.

Shareholders often get the short end of the profit stick. Shareholders are at the bottom of the corporate pyramid and they control very little. The Securities and Exchange Commission lately has been compelling corporations to make more inside financial information available. While this is helpful to security analysts and big investors, relatively few shareholders know what to do with this information when they get it.

The balanced truth about American businesses is that most executives are responsive to government legislation and control and do the best they can for their customers, employees, and shareholders. But there have been too many scandals for anyone studying the business scene to ignore the many against-the-public-interest shortcuts some executives take in their quest to fatten up their corporation's bottom line of profit.

Why are people so hostile to business?

You ask, "Why are so many people so openly hostile to American business?" I offer these answers:

1. American business executives can't escape all of the blame.

2. American business executives in general do not feel it is anyone's business how they run their company. Some wish *The Wall Street Journal,* Reuter's, the business editors of newspapers, and the spirited editors of business and financial magazines would stop snooping and print only what the executives give them.

3. Americans, on the other hand, have become far more knowledgeable about what makes business tick than did those in previous generations. The young people of today are less inclined to treat top businessmen as infallible gods. They ask tougher questions and demand better information and more adequate treatment. They sincerely question and challenge the

system, regardless of the raised eyebrows and expletives of old-time employees who have become accustomed to their plantation-boss existence.

4. Business has been "exposed" many times, and accurately to some degree, by consumer groups, environmental groups, clean-air-and-water groups, unions, newspaper writers, TV documentaries, and even a few good movies. They've also been flushed out by lawsuits which have sent many an embarrassed president scuttling to the protection of his staff of lawyers. Some of these "exposure" actions have been unjustified harassment. Others have been based on a definite premise that something is wrong in a company's actions and needs to be corrected.

5. Despite these sensational charges against business leaders, the basic truth is that hostility toward them comes, not from the bad things some of them do, *but from their general lack of good communications about the good things most of them do.*

Anyone expecting all business executives to be Mr. Clean just isn't with it. But anyone expecting all executives to be Mr. Dirt is much more asinine. Business leaders who have *told* their employees what is going on, who have interpreted company events and actions, have found that employees react favorably.

Business executives in general have done enormously well in providing security to their people. They have raised the standard of living of Americans to the highest in the world. They have contributed vast resources to social, civic, educational, and recreational endeavors. The sum of the technology they have developed and their aggressiveness has taken the United States from an agricultural economy to a world power in all major areas.

I can't say enough about the good things business executives have done for America and its people. Certainly there have been many cases of inept management, of skullduggery, of misuse of power, and all that. But these have been outweighed by far by the fantastic contributions made to all of us by the men and women who run our free enterprise system.

Still, when you reduce these good and bad factors to the level of "boss" and "bossed," you find that this one-on-one area still needs much work to effect good changes. The concept that has snagged too many people still exists everywhere, and it critically needs attention.

Let's go back to our sharp examination of bosses and the role they play in inhibiting you or in propelling you upward.

Why does anyone want to be a boss?

Why would *you* want to be a boss?

1. Security is the number one reason. It is better to boss than to be bossed.

2. Ego satisfaction is another strong reason. It appeals more to some people to be recognized as a leader rather than as a follower.

3. Drive, personal initiative, desire for achievement, and a need for recognition as a doer all combine to motivate many people to want to become bosses. As bosses they can find a wider outlet for these emotional pushes.

4. Status, money, title, larger benefits, and plushier work surroundings are self-interest goals which stimulate others to become bosses.

Psychologists tell us there are many reasons why men and women want to be bosses. I know some people would say, "Do I have to have a reason to want to be a boss?" No one tries to become a boss of other people unless that person has some selfish reason, or multiple selfish reasons. Selfishness is undeniably a basic human characteristic.

Give yourself a little test right now. Why would *you* want to become a boss, assuming that you are not one now? You'll come up with a standard, basic reason that most people will give in answer to this question. "I would feel better if I were the boss. I would do the job better, and it would lead to better things."

See? You want to "better" yourself. So does everyone who now is a boss. Selfishness is terrible if it's exhibited by someone else but acceptable if *you* exhibit it. Isn't that the case?

What do bosses want most?

They want what you want, perhaps more.

Almost all bosses have two major objectives:

1. To keep the job they have.

2. To get a higher job with more money, prestige, and side benefits.

These are very human goals. The difference is that a boss has more things to *lose* than you have. This makes a boss more protective, more edgy, more nervous, and more easily disturbed when things happen that might pose a threat to the boss's security. That's why most bosses can never forgive insubordination. Insubordination is an implied threat.

A threat to a boss's security is like a threat to yours—it is taken seriously. The last thing you want to be viewed as by your boss is a threat to his or her security.

You're on your way somewhere else when that happens.

Understanding your boss's actions

Your boss has ways of telling you things without saying a word. If Mr. Boss calls you into his office and closes the door, he has told you one of two things:

A. He is in a pleasant frame of mind and has something confidential to tell you. He is, by closing the door against "the others," telling you he regards you as a safe intimate. You're in good shape.

B. If he is in a dour mood and you can see that he is disturbed, he is saying to you, "I'll trap you in here and enforce my power over you." His closing the door signals that he isn't really sure of his ground and he doesn't want anyone else to hear what he is going to say. He probably feels guilty, and his closing the door puts him on firmer ground. Your ground isn't so firm.

If he comes into *your* office and starts talking to you, but not looking at *you,* he is saying, "I'm just doing this to show I'm a nice guy. I'd rather have you in my office where I can control you better."

He hands you an assignment and says, "There's no hurry about it. Fit it into your schedule wherever you can." What he means is, "Drop everything and get to work on it." When he says, "Things like that never bother me," he is really saying, "That gripes the hell out of me."

Do bosses tell the truth? Not always. Example: Boss Elmer announces a strict campaign to cut costs of the group. He goes after it like a beaver. Actually, there is no crying need to cut costs more than normal. Boss Elmer is just trying to make himself look good to *his* boss. He wants to be seen as a man who gets things done, a watchdog who makes tough decisions and carries them out. He's using the group to further his own ambitions. Does he tell the group this?

Understanding your boss's actions isn't difficult if you make an effort to look behind what the boss *says.* It is what the boss *does* that is important. Actions are more important than words. Words often are camouflage or window dressing. Actions are deliberate and undeniable. You gain a sharper insight into your boss when you study the boss's actions than when you accept solely what is said.

Do you deal your boss four aces?

Like many others, you may be ascribing more powers to Ms. Boss than she actually has. It's like deliberately dealing her four aces. "Look, here are the cards. Take the whole pot!" Why people do this is a mystery, but there is plenty of evidence that it is done. I can offer some opinions.

1. When we're young, we have parents and older people around us. They are bigger and wiser, and we're in their power until we're old enough and big enough to get off on our own.

2. When we had "kid jobs," we had bosses who supervised us and we learned that if we displeased them, we got fired or drew the sticky assignments.

3. In school we had teachers; they had authority over us because they knew so much more than we did.

4. When we entered the business world, we quickly learned that if the boss liked us, we could get raises and better working conditions.

The temptation to ascribe more power to your boss than the boss actually has is rooted in our fear of being fired, or demoted, or blocked if we cross the boss. This is good thinking because that is usually what happens.

On the other hand, we're bowing to a *fear*, aren't we? The fear of being fired is built into all of us because it represents a terrible personal failure. We're all horror-stricken about failing.

Isn't it silly to worry about something that *hasn't* happened and probably never will? The fear keeps us from speaking our mind at times when we know we should speak up. We keep our mouths shut because we feel the boss wouldn't like what we have to say and will react against us. Instead, we say what we think the boss wants to hear, and we're disgusted with ourselves. The fear keeps us from going in to see the boss with an idea we regard as worthy of consideration. The boss might not like it, or so we think.

For the same reason we don't go in and bargain for better working conditions, for less work when we're overloaded, for more equipment or budget to do our assignments more accurately and efficiently. In short, we've made the boss a fearful object. That's the last thing most progressive bosses want to be. They want ideas and suggestions. They need your help.

Granted, some of them turn away a lot of good ideas and suggestions. The point is, it is your job to help your boss, against the boss's will at times.

If you've got something to say, or want something from your boss, go in and work it out. Don't make the boss bigger and more fearsome than any boss is or has a right to be. If the boss is wrong, point out where the mistake is and offer constructive information.

Don't deal your boss four aces from under the deck. Make your boss play whatever cards fall on the table, as the rest of us must do.

Have some heart for the executive biggies

In relation to everyone else, the president and the chairman of the board are usually isolated from the nitty-gritty of getting things done around the corporation. They spend their time in planning, trying to look into the future, worrying about the bid and ask features of the stock, fighting off the crushes of the competition, and coping with government regulations.

They're not lonely people, although many articles have tried to leave this impression. They have numerous meetings and conferences, mostly with the highest-level people in the corporation, attorneys, tax experts, acquisition experts, bankers, insurance executives, international experts, and their own top vice presidents and general managers. Every day is well filled.

If they are lonely, it is that they are frequently out of touch with their own people, their own corporation. They carry their mantle of power with perhaps too much stateliness. They feel that the ordinary person should be kept away from them so that they can attend to the critical business of running the little empire.

Those who have studied the upper echelon of executives say that it isn't all a breeze. It is difficult being the "big boss." It is hard to keep making profits rise year after year. The experts say that the top executives of American business as a group lose their jobs at a comparatively dramatic rate because they fail to get the "bottom line" the board of directors want.

So have a little heart for the executive biggies. It's not all that easy up there, nor is there all that much job security.

Cherries on top of the whipped cream

Did you know that Mr. Boss and his peers, if they are considered executives, probably have some, if not all, of these benefits in addition to their salaries and large offices?

1. A company car with all expenses paid, including gas, oil, parking, maintenance, and sometimes even a chauffeur

2. Country club memberships

3. Business, university, or athletic club memberships

4. Trade association memberships

5. Stock options (they can buy at a lower price than you can)

6. Cash bonuses, if the corporation's sales or earnings pass, specified goals set by the board of directors

7. Assistance in buying large and impressive houses suitable to their station in life

8. Attendance at special events, usually held in the name of a business program but where playing golf or poker is the big attraction

9. Contracts which assure them of pay raises and bonuses up to their retirement time and perhaps even keep them on the payroll for years in the event they are booted out in favor of others

10. Agreements which guarantee that their children will attend certain universities under scholarships paid for by the corporation

Top executives enjoy many unusual and expensive privileges far out of proportion to those of the average person, who gets a meager vacation, receives only carefully controlled pay raises, and lives by a tough book of dos and don'ts governing each work day.

The day-after-day struggle on the job

Each day, the same boss, the same scene, the same supporting cast of characters. The repetitious nature of some jobs can make them a boring Dullsville. The excitable nature of other jobs makes them a constant panic zone which tries the souls of those who hold them. There are yet others where the usual peace and tranquillity of the work are shattered by occasional crises and disruptions.

Whatever your job, you have opportunities that fall in your lap and you have opportunities that you make yourself. If you have a boring job, it's because you allow it to be boring. If you have a crisis-prone job, it's because you choose to stay and deal with the crises.

Each day when you show up for work, say to yourself these two things: "What can I do to do my job better?" and "What can I do today to help my boss?" What you are saying, in effect, is, "What can I do to help me get ahead faster?"

Each day make a list of the things you want to do to put more zip into your job and help you achieve more. Make a list of the things you can do to help your boss. Tackle the lists and do whatever you can. Leave room for unexpected events that disrupt you or sidetrack you. They will happen.

Even with the same boss, the same scene, and the same cast, you can make progress every day on the job.

What you owe to yourself in the business world

What is *really* important to you in connection with your job? Security? Money put away in the bank or in stocks, bonds, and real estate? Having power, prestige, extra benefits?

You are not one of those people who want to grind away every day at the same work, year after year, disliking the job intensely. You are most concerned with getting satisfaction out of your job, with feeling significant, necessary, capable, and in charge of your own life. You are concerned with doing work that pleases you, gives you a feeling of personal achievement, and gives you some of the security that you and your family need.

Many older, single-career people trusted the corporation to take care of them. They learned that corporation management changes, sometimes very frequently and dramatically. They learned that, while older corporation policies spell out benefits to them, some of the newer executives coming in feel the older employees are owed nothing by them.

These employees came to understand, possibly too late in life to do them much good, that they always had the opportunity to take charge of their own careers, to be in charge of their own life in the business world, and not to rely solely on the company. You have learned that *already*. You're ahead of the game.

If you begin to feel restless in any job, you don't have to remain in it. Talk it over with your boss. If you get nowhere with the boss, start looking around for the type of job you want, the thing you really want because you get enjoyment out of it. You owe yourself dignity and a chance to be *you* in the business world.

What you owe to yourself is your life. Don't let any corporation or other organization lead you into a blind path. You know what pleases you. Go out and get the job that suits you, not some organizational chart. There's a saying, "A job is *you* at the moment." Your best type of job is one that gives you some of the important things you want out of life. Wearing a wrong job is like wearing clothes that are absolutely uncharacteristic of you.

Being unhappy in any job is easy if the job doesn't fit your personality and your desires. Why be unhappy? Money isn't worth it. No matter how difficult or troublesome it may appear, cut yourself loose from your blind-path job and get into a field where you're more at home, where there is the type of satisfaction you like to achieve.

Perhaps you'll work longer hours and have less money, but you'll be happier. Happiness is what you owe yourself, and you get that most when you're doing what you like best.

Which way to look?
A way out, a way up?

"Don't look for a way out, look for a way up." A self-made millionaire told me this one day, and I've never forgotten it. The trouble with good advice is that it is so hard to keep in mind all of the time.

We all look for an easy way to win things for ourselves. It's a very human method, but it doesn't always work for us. What does work is coming to grips with what is bothering us and looking for a way up.

Another way of saying this used to be, "Every cloud has a silver lining." Psychologists tell us that we do our best when we have some pressure on us. The pressure can be from within, or it can be from your boss, your group, or your family. Each crisis holds a lot of pressure for you and opportunities as well.

A few paragraphs ago, we talked about leaving a job that had become a dead end for you and looking for one which would gain you the recognition and feeling of being significant that are so essential. But if your job is *not* a dead end, only troublesome, then in the midst of all of the difficulties *there may be a way up for you.*

What is bothering you will normally make you discontented, and you'll consider making a move to another company. Before you make the move, look carefully at the situation. Are you missing an opportunity to move in on the difficulties, apply your skills and efforts, and solve some of the difficulties?

Many an executive became so by moving in on troubles and

setting things right. It's hard work, touchy work, but, if you have the guts to move in on what's bothering you, you may also be moving up.

What to expect from your present job?

Let's see what you think you can do with your present job.
From my present job I expect:
- To be president of my organization
- To become a top executive
- To become a top manager
- To be fully vested in my company's profit-sharing fund
- To be protected by the retirement plan
- To use it as a stepping-stone to something much better
- To learn as much from it as I can so that I can get off on my own as a small business person
- Just a paycheck every month
- Nothing but disappointment, because the system is all wrong for me
- To be blocked in progress, and I'll soon have to make a move to somewhere else

Did these statements tell you anything about yourself? You should know what your present job can do for you. You should have a path charted which will take you to where you want to go in the business world.

Think a bit about these questions. Are you settling for less? Are you on the right track? What must you do to make your present job more satisfying and more rewarding in success?

Think, and then get busy doing something about it.

Leave the office in a cheerful mood

Experts who study the business world have told us for years that we should not "take the office home" with us. This is easier said than done. Most of us get wrapped up in our little corner of the business establishment, and it takes us some time to unwind and forget what happened during the day. Particularly is this so if the boss jumped on us, or if a coworker messed things up, or if some small calamity popped up in our midst.

There is a method of leaving the office, or plant, behind when we beat a hasty exit. It doesn't work every day, but it is worth working on. Here are the elements:

1. A half-hour before quitting time make a list of the things you want to tackle the next working day. Assign a priority to them. What will help your boss most? What will help *you* most?

2. Straighten your desk or work area; put things away.

3. Lean back in your chair and say to yourself, "I've done my work as well as I could today. I learned a few new things from my boss and the others. I have a lot to do when I get back here. I'll try to do everything better."

4. Then tell yourself that "taking the office home" will probably make you moody and take the edge off of the *time that you have coming to yourself.*

The reason you work is so that you can afford your own personal life. By taking the office home with you when it is not highly essential, you're voluntarily surrendering hours of your own freedom. Why do you want to do that? Leave the office in a cheerful mood, knowing the work will be there waiting for you when you get back.

Have you changed your "boss" and "bossed" concept?

You are not powerless. The boss does not have all of the power. No one controls you but yourself. The fact that you report to a boss doesn't mean that you lose any freedom of speech or freedom of choice.

If you have learned those facts in this chapter, then you have changed your concept of "boss" and "bossed." You do not have to fear any boss. You can work with a bad boss, a good boss, a second-rate boss—any boss—and make a great deal of progress for yourself in the business world.

No boss takes away your freedom of choice. No boss takes away your initiative and your desire to succeed. No boss puts you in the freezer and keeps you there. *No boss does anything to you unless you allow it.*

In the chapters ahead, we will examine some of the methods by which you can work more effectively with your boss. In return, you will see how much more you can gain for yourself.

Let's repeat it: the gold mine of success is there for you. You won't find it by surrendering your rights to a boss through a mistaken concept that the boss is all-powerful and *you* are a captive. You'll find nothing but depression by remaining "bossed." Why do that to yourself?

You deserve everything that you're willing to work hard for.

3

Your Role in Creating Better Bosses

As we've seen, all of the power isn't in the hands of the bosses. Some of it is in your hands. You can help make or break a boss. You can work all on your own to assist your boss in going places or you can gang up with others in your group to make a very sticky situation for your boss.

You play a definite role in creating better bosses. It is an uncontested fact that the business world needs a huge number of "better" bosses. We mean better in comparison with the bosses of ten and twenty years ago. They must be more capable today and in the years ahead to handle the workload, which is becoming increasingly more complicated and difficult.

A president of a chemical company told me, "I don't know where we're going to get all of the people we need to manage our business. We have a lot of fine managers, but many of them are not equipped to take on greater responsibilities. It also takes a very long time to turn a university graduate into the kind of a manager that we require for the future."

In this chapter we'll look at the problems the business world has in getting or creating effective bosses and the role that you play in this essential process.

Bosses are the business world's main foundation

Any business must be broken down into hundreds and thousands of separate jobs, each with a purpose. One of these jobs is yours. Another is that of your boss.

In the organization chart, your boss is part of the structural foundation. Executives like to use terms such as "lower-echelon management," "middle management," and "upper-echelon management." You can interpret these terms this way: the first is a boss job which requires little training and can be done by virtually anyone with a little get-up-and-go; the second requires good training and skills; and the third includes the group of bosses who rose quite high and are considered very talented and successful.

From the upper-echelon management come nearly all of the executives, either brought up within an organization or stolen from another corporation by the lures of more money and more power. Traditionally, a person can start a job with a company and work up through this typical chain of command to an executive spot. But in many organizations there is so much movement, so much fluidity of people, that often there are no such clear lines. The game is played the way the cards fall. Some people jump from first to third very quickly. Others who should have been rewarded are passed over.

The greatest asset a corporation has is that group of people who possess continuity with the ways and methods of the company. Few people step right in and take over a keystone job. It takes time to absorb details, practices, and objectives and to become acquainted with the people who surround the job.

Bosses who have been in the harness for five, ten, and fifteen years with the same corporation are prized highly. These are the strongest ingredients of the corporation's foundation.

What the business world
wants of its many bosses

There is a constant upward movement in that foundation. Granted, some bosses remain at one job level a long time. Most of them move upward, creating room for *you* to take one of their places. No foundation is strong if there are gaps or open holes in it. So there are always opportunities coming along for *you*, particularly if your corporation is on the move and not stagnating.

To be moved up, a boss must meet some standard requirements of the executives at the top. These standards vary a bit from company to company, from organization to organization, but basically the variations are minor. What the business world wants of its many bosses includes these skills:

1. *A self-starter capacity* which means the boss doesn't have to be prodded constantly from above to get going.

2. *An ability to get things done* often against a strict time limitation and other difficulties.

3. *The ability to save money* by preventing waste of employees' time, corporation materials, and blocks of effort that go into unfinished or aborted assignments, by avoiding unnecessary programs that pour money down a hole.

4. *The ability to make decisions* of picking a course of action to be taken and then doing something about it.

5. *The ability to make a profit* the most essential skill of all, because corporations are in the business of making money.

A boss who meets these requirements is on the way up and certainly deserves to be promoted.

What the future looks
like for bosses

If there were a single book available to you which would show you the massive endeavor by business organizations, and by business management training associations, to raise the level of all bossdom, you would be amazed. There is nearly a frantic nationwide endeavor going on to train bosses for the challenges of the years ahead. This endeavor has some significant meanings for *you*.

In its simplest meaning, management is rapidly becoming a lot more demanding than ever before. Technology is one reason. Corporations are getting bigger, for another. American life styles are changing at a faster pace, and this is causing shock waves through many business enterprises.

To meet these serious changes, business is backing and strongly encouraging many more comprehensive training classes for its bosses, to equip them with more skills and broader outlooks. The trade associations which operate in those bosses' particular segment of the business world have numerous study groups in operation. Universities offer night classes. Some bosses are even given months to take full-time courses in their areas of interest. There is a strong push to have many persons attend the MBA night courses conducted by universities, usually over a two-year period.

Bosses who take advantage of all this academic or professional training have a very good future in store for them.

You can help your boss move up

A boss moves up when her or his record looks good to the people at the top. *You* can help your boss move up by helping establish the type of record that looks good. Helping your boss is in your self-interest. You've already seen the wisdom of that. A boss who moves up leaves a position that must be filled by another competent person. *That could be you.*

You help your boss go on to bigger things by doing all you can in areas such as these:

1. Being innovative, bringing ideas and suggestions to your boss for cutting waste and making more profits.

2. Getting your work done on time.

3. Playing as much of a role as possible in the decision-making process so that the right decision is made—in other words, contributing your views on how a problem can be solved.

4. Being on time and cutting your absenteeism to an absolute minimum.

5. Being dependable when you're given an assignment, doing it in the professional way the boss wants it done in order to reach an objective.

6. Doing what you can to provide accurate feedback so that your boss knows how things are going.

7. Acting as a smoother for any minor irritations and abrasiveness that spring up within your group.

8. Selling yourself to your boss so that you earn the boss's trust and respect. This is the key to your being selected for the next promotion. You are establishing your own good record.

You can play havoc with your boss's plans

A boss with a record of dissension in the ranks, of difficulties in getting things done, will have a problem getting promoted. Under certain circumstances, you may *not* want your boss to succeed. You may want to see that person moved out of the company or perhaps laterally to another group.

You can play havoc with your boss's plans if you do the following types of things:

1. Delay whatever assignments your boss gives you and use the old ploy, "It takes time!"

2. Fail to understand what the assignment was, go off on another course, and then say, "You didn't make it clear to me!"

3. Never go to your boss with a fresh idea or suggestion.

4. Never contribute your views in a meeting.

5. Ask the boss time and time again, "What did you mean by this or that?"

6. Start new tidbits into the rumor mill about unflattering things you've noticed or heard about your boss.

7. Look for new ways to frustrate your boss by slowing down or blocking the work of others in your group.

8. Complain to your boss's superior that the boss is insensitive, unreasonable, and overly demanding.

This sort of thing can boomerang on you if you're not careful. When it works and you're not caught, it does play havoc with your boss's plans to move ahead.

How Old Frightful became a boss

Your Mr. Boss was "one of us" a few years ago. How did he manage to become a boss of other people? Try this checklist on your boss.

My boss became a boss because:

____He had talent and it was recognized.

____He worked hard and earned it.

____His footwork was faster than his competitors'.

____He has charisma but not much on the ball.

____He had relatives in high places.

____He toadied to his own boss.

____He backstabbed his way in.

____He plotted and schemed for years, and it worked.

____He outlived everyone else.

____He had money to begin with.

____He talked faster than anyone else.

You've analyzed your boss by the Fickle Observer method, and you have some idea of *how* he got to where he is. What rating do you give him as he is right now?

____Abysmal

____Cool cat

____Mediocre

____A disaster

____A winner

_____A grandstander

_____A genius

_____A toady

_____A manipulator

_____Harsh, dictatorial

_____Stiff-necked, unyielding

_____Reasonable, understanding

_____Devious, mysterious

_____Egotistical, self-lover

_____Level-headed

_____A leader

_____Unapproachable

_____Swell person

Somewhere in this checklist you saw your boss emotionally. Perhaps you've been genuinely objective. I mixed up the descriptions so that there wouldn't be any pattern you could follow. What you check is what you believe. To you, that _is_ your boss.

Now you can see how you feel about Old Frightful. Don't be worried about how you feel about your boss. Your boss will never know unless you tell. And who's going to do a thing like that?

How a nice person made it to bossdom

When Harold graduated from Northwestern University he became a management trainee of a large electrical appliance company. At first all he wanted to do was "get established." He listened to all of the scuttlebutt about the company. The groaners said it cared little for people; its bigness dehumanized the employees; it exploited its people and cheated its shareholders.

Harold had three things going for him: he liked to work, he liked people, and he was inquisitive. After several years on the job, getting used to things, a plan formed in his mind. It worked this way:

1. The company wasn't as bad as the complainers made it out. There was plenty of room for advancement. Inescapably, he noticed how many employees and bosses weren't really trying.

2. He set his sights on becoming a divisional vice president. He obtained all of the literature and reports that he could on every division in the company. He kept up with everything printed. He made friends with the publicity department and was placed on the internal list to get news releases, copies of speeches, and other promotional materials.

3. He went to his boss with ideas and suggestions for getting things done faster, more efficiently, and with savings of time and money.

4. He got all of his assignments done well within the time limits and asked the boss for more.

5. It never occurred to him not to be nice to everyone. He spent time with his coworkers, at coffee breaks and lunch time, and got to know them well. He avoided the Gloomy Gus and Bitchy Barbara types and gravitated to those who shared his enthusiasm for work and the company. He was nice to receptionists, switchboard operators, mail room boys, and cafeteria employees.

6. After his first promotion, junior-grade type, he married. He took work home only when it was absolutely necessary, feeling that his wife was as important to him as was his job. He planned his days so that he got the major part of his work done. When he needed help, he asked for it and usually got it.

7. In meetings he spoke up when he had something to contribute.

8. He kept his boss informed of his progress; when he met a roadblock, he went in and discussed it with the boss, and between them they developed methods of overcoming the problem.

9. His second promotion made a boss out of him, with a dozen people reporting to him. He studied each of them and worked, not on a group method, but on an individual person-by-person method. He knew their good and bad features. He helped them in their particular areas of self-interest. He accepted them as they were and helped them everywhere he could, and his group functioned very well.

10. Because he kept up with the *entire company*, not his division alone, he soon became known for his broad approaches and management successes.

At this writing, Harold is a profit center manager in the division, well on his way to someday being the divisional vice president he has set out to be.

Nice people do win.

How another nice person launched a good career

Joan didn't go to college because her family couldn't afford it. All through high school she'd had part-time jobs, helping out the family. She found a job with a big Chicago department store that had satellite stores in a number of the suburbs. Her first years on the job were difficult and she had all she could handle just working for a living.

One day her boss fell ill; she was in a hospital for two weeks. Joan was put in charge of the clothing department on a temporary basis. "The store manager must have crossed his fingers," she told me. "There was so much to learn in such a short time. I hadn't realized the things my boss was responsible for."

Joan survived. She did very well, but she had noticed several important things that previously had escaped her. When her boss returned, Joan went to her. "Couldn't we do these things to pep up sales and help the customers?" she said. The boss agreed. The department began to take off. The store manager became aware of this progress and was pleased with a report from Joan's boss which said, "This young lady has excellent possibilities. She knows how to handle customers, she's not self-centered or petty, she's learning merchandising, and she knows how to help me."

When an opening came in another new store, heading a large women's clothing department, it was offered to Joan. She accepted, and today she has a chance to become a store manager herself one day.

Nice people do win.

The fashion of taking cheap shots at bosses

Taking cheap shots at their bosses is a way of life with many people in the business world. Any boss draws a lot of attention because of the high-visibility area in which bosses exist. Nearly everything a boss does is seen or heard by someone.

You're above this sort of thing—taking cheap shots at your boss. The temptation is great, but the rewards are dismally poor. You're there as an observer, not a two-bit critic. Observing means you are learning. Low-level criticism means you are snipping at the fabric that holds people together in a business organization, the fabric of trust, faith, and cooperation.

There will always be people who carp and sneer about their boss. You don't have to be one of them. Harold and Joan weren't. Why lower yourself to bleacher-seat catcalls when what you want to be doing is raising yourself to the level of your boss and higher?

Go up, not down.

Ways to make your boss a more effective manager

Every boss would like to have your interest in his or her goals, your loyalty, your cooperation in meeting the group's objectives, your well-thought-out ideas and suggestions about cutting waste motion and increasing profits. Is that too much to ask?

Not if the boss deserves it. Here are a number of ways in which you can go about making a more effective manager of your boss:

1. *On the objective level*   Your boss had to have something on the ball to have been put in charge of your group. What are the boss's strong points? How can you help take advantage of these strong points to help the boss achieve greater success? What are the boss's weak points in management? What can you do to help close these gaps?

2. *On the subjective level*   What are your emotions about your boss? Do you feel goodwill, indifference, hostility? Do these emotions come from things the boss does and says? Do they come from you, because the boss doesn't meet your expectation or because the boss turns you off in some way? Are you controlling these emotions? How can you develop more good feelings about your boss?

3. *Equating the self-interests*   You know what your boss wants and what the boss's good and bad features are. *You know what you want.* How do you match the two together?

4. *You make the effort*   You decide the boss *is your business*. You support the boss in the right activities. You express your views when you feel strongly that the boss is headed in the wrong direction. You don't sit back and let the boss succeed or fail all alone. You become *involved* with the boss's goals and objectives. In short, you assume some measure of the boss's responsibility by making the group's work more efficient and more result-producing.

It's easy to be offended by a boss. It's easy to get your feelings ruffled and for you to hold a grudge. After all, the boss is making more money than you are and has more prestige. Why should you go out of your way to help your boss become a better manager? *Because it helps you.* The boss is buying, and you are selling, the help needed for the boss's success.

The better a manager your boss becomes, the more your group prospers and the greater the opportunities you have to prosper as well. Listen to what Eric told me. Eric was a boss. Now he is an executive. This is what he said: "I didn't realize it at the time, but when I first became a boss I was doing all of the wrong things. I was so anxious to succeed that I pushed people around, made them angry with me, and got plenty angry myself at their lack of help."

What happened to make Eric a better manager? "One of the fellows in the group never seemed to be bothered about what I did or said. He kept coming to me with his ideas. I thought he sure had his nerve. After all, I was the boss. Then it began to sink in what he was trying to do. He was trying to help me. I began to listen. I began to try out some of his ideas. He never let me down on an assignment. I got a good look at my errors through his eyes. I responded by trying to be more compassionate, more understanding of others. I took them all into consideration as individuals. I began helping them. Funny how it worked out. My job became more fun. As a group we got more work done and we did it better. One of the girls in the group started to help me in the group's budgeting, where I was weak, and in a year or so we had a really cooperative bunch of guys and gals. It made a world of difference to me."

It certainly did. Eric was promoted, and he naturally recommended the fellow who had first set out to help make Eric a more effective manager. All bosses aren't perfect. Some must be helped in spite of themselves. In their candid moments, executives will tell you how much they owe to the men and women along the way who helped fashion them into more attractive material for promotion.

When you help your boss, don't expect a lot of visible gratitude. Don't expect instant approval of your actions. But in the long run the good things you do to help your boss will prove to be things you did to help yourself.

And isn't that what you're trying to do?

What business trends
mean to your chances

Few companies are in a static position. The vast majority of them are in a constant state of change. New products, new services, new challenges in the marketplaces, changes in what Americans want and no longer want, inflation, pollution, government regulation, social and economic changes of vast proportions, all affect any business organization. Executives and managers are on the go as never before—witness the amount of business air travel and the innumerable business meetings outside of the office.

There is a large turnover of boss positions. There are thousands of new boss positions opening up for the first time. Early retirement is freeing even more bossdom spots. The demand that many corporations conform to state and federal equal employment acts has opened more bossdom chairs for women and minority groups.

The growth of shopping centers has created many more retailing management jobs. The resurgence of service functions has opened up even more opportunities for managers. In addition, few business organizations operate at peak efficiency with a perfect person in every management spot. There is, everywhere, a need for good managers, for people who can get the work done satisfactorily and on time.

Wherever you are, don't feel there is no room for you. It is up to you to fashion yourself into the type of productive person who can be promoted into bossdom. No one is holding you back except yourself. If you are seriously inclined to want to succeed in the business world, the route is clear.

You can be one of those "better bosses" we've been talking about. You can be one of the finest. It is all up to you and your constant application of your talents to continually develop yourself.

Results you can expect in
making your boss a friend

There are three levels of results you can expect from your efforts to make your present boss a friend. They are as follows:

1. *The maximum results* The boss becomes a one-hundred-percent friend and booster of yours, opens new doors for you, helps you increase your managerial powers and develop your talents, and promotes you to better-paying levels of responsibilities. *You win!*

2. *The average results* You catch the boss's interest. Things between you improve. There is no immediate benefit in the area of pay increases or promotions but the opportunities for these are greatly increased. You feel more vital, more respected, more a part of things. *Hope is greater.*

3. *The minimum results* You've reduced the chances for abrasion and hostility between you and your boss. *This* boss might not be the one to open new doors for you, but work becomes a bit more livable—more free—and you are less uptight. You've learned more about the psychology of working with bosses. Perhaps in the near future this applied boss psychology will work more effectively for you—with another boss.

You're not a loser in any of these levels.

Your boss isn't your enemy,
your wrong emotions are

A newspaper story reported that more than 10 million Americans have ulcers. People, it would seem, are eating themselves up in a wave of hopelessness, frustration, and depression. Emotions can do terrible things to you.

Take *depression*. It comes to you when you can't resolve a problem that has created stress for you. You find that the more you struggle to solve the problem, the greater the stress becomes. The enemy here certainly isn't your boss; it's psychosomatic illness caused by the stress you feel when you struggle with problems, or work situations, that are over your head. You simply are expecting too much of yourself, and your defenses are wearing very thin.

Stress, the researchers point out, is the manner in which your body reacts to your uncertain state of mind. Your body is at war with your mind. Your mind tells you that you're not doing as well as you deserve or could under other circumstances. You resent the problem you're trying to resolve. Your body reacts with an illness, even an ulcer.

How do you cope with psychosomatic illness from stress? You have four choices: accept the situation and live with it, draw a line and say you've had enough and will take no more, run away from whatever is causing the problem, or, lastly, root out the source of the problem and clobber it.

If you can't get along with your boss, and you feel the boss is the *source* of the problem that is creating stress for you, you might try what a friend of mine did. She went to her boss and said to him: "I want you to know several things about me. First, I have always appreciated myself. I believe I am a substantial person and an excellent employee of this company. I am not afraid of you in any way, shape, or form. I made my way in life long before you became my boss, and I will continue to do so long after you no longer are my boss. I am not worried in the least whether you accept me or not. I have accepted myself, and that is what is important to me."

Did it work for her? She said it did, and I believe her. Things improved and her stressful situation disappeared in short time. The boss became a better boss because of her straightforwardness. A woman like that is never going to get an ulcer. *Why should you?*

4

The New Ms. and Her Boss

One of the most fascinating and long-overdue changes in the business world involves the new Ms. and her boss. There has been so much publicity about the unshackled woman that one almost has the impression that they just now have invaded the business world. Hardly. Women have been a mainstay of business from the days back when our free enterprise system had its roots in the colonies.

It's a rare business organization that has no women in it. Women are not newcomers to business. There are industries where women represent from 15 to 80 percent of the total work population.

Equal rights legislation prohibits discrimination against women, as well as against other minority groups, in business organizations. Business executives deny deliberate discrimination. They used to point out that most women aren't "inclined by nature" to become bosses or executives. Now they still talk about myths as if they were real. The fact that many women have excellent university educations and substantial experience in the business world still doesn't convince some of these hard-line executives.

The business world is opening up rapidly for competent women—not just to make grudging room for them, but because they *deserve the right to become bosses and executives on their own merits.* There are *already* countless successful business women, and more are on their way up. Some men don't like this situation because jobs once held exclusively by men are now being held by women.

In a few business organizations some critical situations have developed because top management, in its collective effort to conform to the federal and state laws, have willy-nilly put women in certain jobs whether they were qualified or not. They want to escape punitive action by the government or discrimination lawsuits. This sort of thing has raised serious criticisms by men who felt they were unjustly deprived of jobs they deserved on the basis of merit.

In big changes resulting from antidiscrimination laws protecting women, and they are big changes, there are bound to be thorny problems arising. In the long run it will all smooth down and women will be able to compete with men more equally without sexism being involved. But don't expect such a happy atmosphere for a long time. You'll have to work for what you get, girls.

The new Ms. will find that being a woman will earn her some consideration, but that over the long haul she'll have to produce work as well as the men. She'll have to fit into the character of the business she's in. The main thing is that women and men are *individuals,* and it will come to the business world sooner or later that job promotions go to the *individuals* who earn them. Women deserve the same right as men to have opportunities for places in any organization, to earn better jobs, to secure better pay.

The more progressive executives see antisexism as a boon to the business world. Let's examine some of the good and bad things about Ms., her boss, and the business world, and why knit pants suits are being seen more frequently along with knit business suits in bossdom.

Farewell to the old office Miss and Mrs.

I asked a woman why she had spent thirty years working at the same dreary job with the same company. She had remarked often about how she hated the work and the discrimination she felt she had been subjected to. Her answer was, "Where else could I go and get a better job?"

Those days seem to be on their way out. Now we read about women who are plumbers, women who are telephone line-persons, women who are welders, women who do high-rise construction work, and women who work in hundreds of other places that once were the exclusive domain of men. Women have proved themselves as magazine editors, authors, doctors, lawyers, nurses, fashion models, actresses, decorating authorities, nutritionists, columnists, and publishers and in scores of other top jobs. They are just as capable as men are of doing outstanding work in the business world.

Older women shake their heads in disbelief at the "Ms." title. Many of them scorn it. Men take it mostly as a joke. Despite this, women's liberation is working, and there is a growing climate for women in the business world, belatedly and a bit shaky at the moment.

Ms. is here to stay, and the impact will be greater on the business world in the years ahead. The impact will result, not from "make jobs" for women, but because women have demonstrated that they can do the work as well as men and can compete for the promotions.

Welcome, Ms.!

The opening world of
women's opportunities

As we've seen, women already have made inroads into the business world. They are bosses and executives, and they do remarkably well. What about the young Ms. just entering the business world?

It isn't going to be a walkaway by any means. The business world is a tough place with a huge burden to carry. It needs competent people, and for the young Ms. to move up, she must be as tough, dedicated, flexible, and responsible as her male counterpart.

With strong legislation on the books to prohibit discrimination, she has a far better chance of making it if she *does* possess the qualifications, shows determination, and constantly prepares herself to take on greater loads of work. She no longer can be held back by such corporate dodges as: The job is in an all-male group and the men don't want a woman in that particular group; a young girl wouldn't stay because probably she'd become married and quit to have a baby; a young girl wouldn't be strong enough to do the same muscular work a man must do in the group.

The 1964 Civil Rights Act, under Title VII, was amended by the 1972 Equal Employment Opportunity Act. The protection provided includes that in private employment no one can be discriminated against because of sex, race, national origin, or religion or because they've gone to an employment agency or joined a union.

Any company with more than fifteen people on the payroll, educational institutions, and state and local governments are prohibited from discriminating against anyone in the areas of salaries and wages, pension and profit-sharing plans, company-funded educational programs, promotions, fringe benefits, and other areas of the work situation.

You've noticed how so many advertisements have at least

one black person included in the illustration and at least one person who is of Latin American extraction? Discrimination is also prohibited in advertising for product sales, for employment openings, and so forth. In short, discrimination of all types is becoming harder to get away with.

Any Ms. entering the business world might find it useful to obtain copies of Title VII, 1964 Civil Rights Act, and the Equal Employment Opportunity Act. Or she may visit or telephone the nearest EEO Commission offices to have her questions answered.

What does all this mean to the Ms. entering the business world? It obviously means that many opportunities are opening up. The biggest hurdle will be for the Ms. to get equal pay for the same work done by men. This is changing slowly, but not as fast as it could be in some business areas. Don't expect absolute adherence to the laws. When you find such laxity, go in and talk to your boss about it. If no one challenges the laxities, why shouldn't business try to get away with them?

Ms., *some* of the responsibility for equal rights is *yours*. Demand them and earn them.

The problems the Ms. has in meeting the business world

Men are *expected* to try to become bosses, to work to move upward to the executive suite. This is so well established that it presents a negative block to women who try to do the same. For a wide variety of reasons it is *not generally expected* of them.

One old-line executive made these points in assessing the problems the young Ms. has in meeting the business world on its terms:

1. Women tend to be more subjective than objective and "take everything personally."

2. They try to use their good looks and cajolery to replace

the necessary persuasion and "talk it out" method widely used among men in groups and committees.

3. While they can take supervision fairly well from men, they resent taking supervision from other women and are unnecessarily more competitive with their own sex.

4. They have trouble coping with male attitudes because they lack the same "training ground" experience the men have had.

5. They inhibit men from properly expressing themselves within the group for fear that honest criticism and personal viewpoints will be considered discriminatory.

The old-line executive was speaking from his position. There are others who will contest his points. There is an element of truth in them all, but they do not apply to every young Ms. entering the business world. What is definitely seen as a critical problem is how to avoid being a "showpiece" in an office (What do you mean, we discriminate? Look at Ms. Jones over there!). Equally critical will be her opportunity to acquire the on-the-job experience which will qualify her for better jobs along the upward line.

Of all the problems, one of the most difficult will be for the young Ms. to adapt her concepts of the business world to what is real. A Ms. who decides to major in business administration in college will find things quite different when she starts to work for a corporation. Men have been finding that out for decades. The academic view of the business world doesn't always square with reality.

Being flexible, adaptable, eager to learn, persuasive, and determined and possessing an enormous ability to be understanding of the problems inherent in business are essential ingredients of a young Ms.'s ability to rise to meaningful jobs in the business world.

As we've said elsewhere, for all problems there are answers. The young Ms. must bring her share of problem-solving, even when she is considered by die-hards to be part of the problem.

Advantages the new Ms. gives the business world

There are thousands of low-level "men only" jobs from which women once were barred. There are thousands of "muscle" jobs which once were held only by men. You, young Ms., assessing your chances of making it in the business world, have some advantages in shooting for a boss's job and later for an executive's job.

The advantages that *you* bring to the hard-bound business world include these:

1. *A fresh viewpoint* Just because men have been making decisions based on their viewpoints for years doesn't mean *you* can't contribute your ideas, suggestions, and evaluations.

2. *New ways of doing things* You aren't as locked in as some men are. You can see things in a different way and you can develop new and better ways of getting work done.

3. *Helping older women* These fine people haven't had the fresh start that you've had. They entered the business world twenty and thirty years ago. They have suffered the problem of doing the same work as men without getting the same pay or treatment. Your new freedom will help them because a business organization can't give you special treatment without doing something for them. In fact, many a corporation is undergoing a sharp reconsideration of its "women" policies.

4. *Opening up new business areas* There is no reason why young women coming into business can't help their company open up new sales opportunities in areas previously considered the domain of men. The Ms. can become a specialized salesperson, or she can develop a sales opening where none existed before. The same holds true in the other areas of the company. Fresh ground can always be broken by anyone with enough determination and innovativeness to do so.

The new Ms. and her ability
to manage others in business

A young woman coming into the business world faces many established practices. Every company has set up certain ways of doing its thing. While these practices are undergoing changes, they seldom change at breathtaking speed. The new Ms. must learn these practices and abide by them until she can offer suggestions for improvement.

In the business world, for a very long time, there has been a search for better ways to manage and motivate people more effectively. It is an unceasing challenge. People *are* the corporation, and it is the output, or productivity, of the people that allows a company to make a profit, stay in business, and grow.

Managing others is a serious challenge. The young Ms. can't say, "This is the way it should be done. Why won't everyone agree?" She has to know what she's talking about and have her suggestion clearly defined and the potential results well worked out.

When she is given the opportunity to manage other people, she needs to use all her skills to get them harmonized with the objectives her superior and she want to achieve. Management of others is never easy, for a man or a woman. It may come a bit easier for the young woman coming freshly into the business world who is the product of a finer, broader education.

Subjective or not, she must remember that she does not own any of the people she manages, nor do they owe her anything she doesn't earn in the way of respect, courtesy, consideration, and support. I've heard a number of businessmen remark, in this or some other way, "The trouble with women as bosses is that they take everything so personally. They want people to cooperate with them just because they are women and not because they have shown the *reasons* for cooperation to their people."

Another complaint along the same line is that women are thin-skinned. "When things go wrong a woman will look for someone to blame, or claim some inanimate object such as a machine caused the problem," another executive said. Taking criticism and responsibility is part of the game, girls, and this must be accepted. Not that some men don't use the same ploys, but a woman is more apparent when doing so!

Managing others, when you're boss, won't be as easy as you think, young Ms. Get yourself prepared to stand up and take it as well as to dish it out. When you're prepared this way, you're on your way to being a better boss.

Understanding the married woman worker in the group

More women than ever before, percentagewise, are working in offices and plants. We've seen that. Many of them are married. They're capable and hard-working, for the most part. They're also doing many of the jobs that once were considered the bailiwick of men. They're getting more money, too. They are changing the old patterns of men versus women in the business world.

The married woman has long been accepted in business. Yet, she has seldom received the attention and opportunities there that she deserves. In addition to being a worker, she's a wife, a mother, a home-keeper, a consumer, a taxpayer, a home nurse, a commuter, and a community contributor.

The married woman might not be motivated to try to go high in the company. She most often wants the job only as another source of income to help her husband, to provide additional security, to obtain more material things, to put children through college, to pay off the mortgage, to pay for medical bills, or the like. Because of this she may accept a job of shattering boredom.

Other married women have outstanding talent and they want to move up to the executive suite. They fight the competitive battle on the same ground as the men, and when they win, it is usually because they have earned the right to be promoted.

There is no basic rule for understanding married women since few are exactly alike. There is, however, a growing understanding in the business world that these fine persons are not just a work pool, but individuals who must be judged on their particular merits, achievements, and skills. I've noticed that married women in offices tend to socialize with other married women, and that the unmarried women have their coffee breaks and lunches with other unmarried women. People of like nature seek each other out, but this in an office tends to polarize the two groups.

Men, on the other hand, don't polarize quite as much. The unmarried male is taken in by the married men. In this sense, the unmarried man has an easier go of it because he doesn't have this particular barrier to break down.

Married women workers constitute a huge mainstay of the American business establishment. They are remarkable persons because they contribute so much skilled effort to the establishment and because they are helping to support their families. None of this is easy, and they deserve far more understanding from business than they've heretofore been given.

But, ladies, better days are coming.

Understanding the single young girl in the group

A lot of men feel that the business world would be bleak and depressing if it weren't for the pretty young girls who brighten up the place. It isn't easy for the pretty young girl. She's new, and there is so much to learn. The older women are a bit envious, perhaps even catty, and they can't be blamed. They like attention, and it's no fun watching the men ogle the younger girls.

Men, whether they're married or not, are attracted to the single young girl. That's something in the establishment that isn't going to be changed, because it's universal. They can't help complimenting her on her hairdo, her dress, her jewelry, her work, or whatever. They can't help looking at her when she walks around the place.

The troublesome aspects of all this for you, the single young girl, include these problems:

1. It is hard for most men to believe that you won't get married in the near future and leave as soon as the first baby is on the way.

2. It is equally difficult for most men to believe that you are serious about wanting to stay and become a boss and later an executive.

3. Most men are not convinced that ideas and suggestions from a pretty young girl have any solid substance, although they often are surprised at the excellent suggestions for work-flow improvement that young girls can make.

4. Men are men-oriented, and they feel their first obligation is to help a man succeed. They feel that if they help a young girl, they will be suspect of being on the make.

5. Most men have no hesitation in recommending a young girl for a slightly higher job if it doesn't interfere with some man's right to the same job. But if the girl strongly indicates she wants more responsibility and more pay in competition to a man, then it becomes another problem.

The fact that more men are "coming around" to accepting young unmarried women as career potentials is heartening. What makes the difference is that young unmarried girls are *earning the right to be promoted* on the basis of their individual business skills and efforts.

What any woman must remember about business

Unmarried or married, all women in the business world must keep in mind some important facts about business. They include:

1. Companies are in the business of making profits.

2. When you are given a job, it is up to you to produce results; you can't look to someone else to do your work.

3. It is important for you to help your boss, man or woman, to achieve the objectives of your group.

4. There is always room for improvement in any area of business. If you have ideas, you are to take them to your boss for examination and possible use.

5. It is up to you to cooperate in cutting down waste of time, effort, and money in order to help your company make reasonable profits.

6. If you are competing against a man, don't rush to raise the scarlet flag of the sexism-discrimination issue; go after the promotion on your own merit.

7. Business is changing, and you'll change along with it. What you feel strongly about today may be nothing to you a few years from now. Remain flexible.

8. Avoid being divisive, turning persons against persons.

9. Work at understanding people not according to their religion, ethnic origin, color, or sex, but as humans with their specific right to be treated as individuals.

Why some bosses keep themselves aloof

One manager told me, "There was this young girl who joined our group. She had talent and worked hard, and I cottoned to her because she did have get-up-and-go power. She reminded me a bit of my oldest daughter. I helped her as much as I could. Then people started to say that I was 'on the make' or that I 'looked like an old fool.' I backed off because some of the people in the group practically had me in bed with her."

Another manager had the opposite story. "I learned years ago to keep my distance from the young men," she said. "People's tongues wag at every little thing. I wanted to put a bit of extra help into several excellent university graduates to speed them along. The extra training would have helped the group, but I was leery of the implications some of the people would put on my efforts. 'Look at her, she's old enough to be their mother. What is she thinking of?' I knew what they'd make out of it and kept more than the normal distance."

If your boss isn't doing all that could be done to help speed *you* on your way, it may be because the boss's help can be easily misunderstood by the dirty minds in your group.

Look for the friend in your very own boss

You have a boss, man or woman. Your boss represents a friend. Your boss is the corridor through which you must pass in order to get higher on the pay scale and gain a more prestigious share of authority in the company. At the risk of overemphasizing the point, let me repeat the basic rules for all women in the business world:

1. Make an effort to understand your boss and the problems your boss must deal with.

2. Make an effort to help your boss solve these problems.

3. Never be afraid of your boss; take in to your boss your plans for solving a particular problem, of improving the work output, of doing things better.

4. Be considerate of your boss instead of hostile or indifferent. Bring yourself into more friendly harmony with your boss rather than building a wall between the two of you.

5. Do your assignments on time and ask for more. If you run into a snag, talk it over right away with your boss. Never let things stew until a real mess results.

In short, act in a responsible, mature manner toward your boss. If your boss is a good boss, you'll be rewarded faster than if he is a bad boss. But even a bad boss will come around to seeing you as an advantage and not a disadvantage. It just takes more time. Either way, you're developing the friendly trust and confidence that prompt your boss to give you promotions, pay raises, and more benefits.

What else are you working for?

The touchiest point: what women are paid

There is an illusion I don't want to create. It is that women suddenly are going to be bringing home big paychecks equal to those that men get. Despite all of the progress women have made in acquiring millions more jobs over the past several decades, in no way, shape, or form have they acquired equally high earnings.

The Bureau of Labor Statistics points out that many jobs held by women are in the lower-paid, less skilled areas. In some companies, the lowest starting salaries for men occur where the highest salaries for women leave off. Women just have not been able to move into many of the areas where high skills gain high pay. This is particularly true in the executive suite and in the upper-level manager echelon.

The Bureau has established that on a nationwide basis men have been paid more for the same work as that done by women. Part of this problem is the attitude this nation has had for many years that "women belong in the kitchen," or that "they should be at home raising the kids," or that "men are the breadwinners, and they deserve more money in order to support their families."

Part of it has been that many women were not well enough educated to hold higher-paying jobs. Another part of it is that women *accepted* the discrimination. They were glad to get any kind of work and any level of pay. While they grumbled and disliked the situation, it has been only in recent years that they have joined together in such a sharp outcry that legislation has been enacted to *enforce* their rights.

I've said it before and I'll repeat it. Young Ms. in the business world, take advantage of all opportunities for further education, night school classes, or whatever is available to you. Obtain the formal education or technical training that you need to qualify for those higher-paying jobs which are held by men because *they* took the trouble to get the education or training.

To the extent that you apply yourself, to the extent that you use your energy and talents to *prepare* yourself for bigger things, you will gain jobs far up the organizational chart. Those jobs have nice price tags on them, but you *must* have the qualifications to hold them.

The executive suites in the business world have relatively few women in them. Those who made it were the ones who were qualified. The same holds true for you, young Ms. Keep working hard to build yourself into the type of person who *deserves* to be promoted that far up the ladder of success.

It's the route men have had to follow, and there is no shortcut for you just because you are a woman. You'll have to earn it, every step of the way.

Good luck! *You can do it if you set your mind to do it.*

5

Fitting Yourself Snugly into the Business World

In the previous pages we looked at the love-hate relationship between you and your boss, how concepts of bossdom are changing, how you can help create a better boss, and how young women are changing some old situations.

Later on we'll explore both the insensitive and the responsive types of bosses, how you can work best with your group, and how you can find that measure of success that you've set out to earn.

Fitting yourself into the business world, which is what this chapter is all about, is never easy. After a while, no matter what jobs you've had, what successes you've scored, you begin to feel pains of doubt about the business world. Dissatisfaction with your rate of progress, disenchantment with business practices, discouragement about office politics, and other deep moods hit you.

"It is virtually impossible to escape the feeling of being turned off about business," said a vice president of a medical equipment company. "The time will arrive when you assess your situation and decide that things simply have not turned out the way you thought they would. The business world is more complicated and difficult than you realized. It is not always a warm, comradely place. Mostly it is cool and unfriendly."

People in the business world are often complex, hard to work with. On top of that, you've not turned out to be the person you thought you were. With all these factors, how can you fit yourself snugly into a world you didn't make and over which you seem to have little or no control?

Let's take a look.

Contemplation over your breakfast coffee

Tomorrow, linger over your coffee at breakfast for an extra minute or two and try these thoughts:

1. It is normal for all of us to feel a painful doubt about the business world. The office or the plant where you work isn't geared to be a totally cheerful, responsive place. It is geared to get work done and to make some money for the owners. *Doubt is normal.*

2. The realities of the business world are tough for all of us to accept. We want to change the place, and we feel we can't make many changes in business practices, systems, and rules. But our common sense tells us that we can make changes if we accept the realities and work within the structure of practicality and not that of pure idealism. *Realities can be accepted.*

3. Your choice this day is between being passive—a spectator—or being active—a player. It is a route of your choice. You gain more by being active, a player. *You make the choice.*

4. What do you want to accomplish on this day? What needs of yours do you want to fill? How can you win things for you?

How can you promote your self-interest? *You come first.*

5. What opportunities can you seize this day and what trouble spots can you avoid? Being prepared before you go to work will work wonders with you. *See the opportunities.*

6. Steady yourself for the day's work. You'll need your sense of perspective, of discipline, to keep you on a straight course. *Control gives you confidence.*

Finish the coffee and go to work.

Forming this day's game plan on your way to work

On your way to work, run over these thoughts in your mind.

1. No one knows your workload better than you do. What are the priority items? What strategy can you develop right now to make this day as productive and as beneficial to you as possible? *Develop your action plan.*

2. What problems can you anticipate? You accept problems as part of the job. You know you can expect some, and others will come out of the woodwork. *Anticipate problems.*

3. What needs to be cleaned up? Assignments left over from the previous work day, some small jobs that have been left unattended, or what? *Do clean up work.*

4. You've spotted some opportunities. A report to the boss. A committee meeting. A special visitor coming in. You'll do better when you're organized mentally to take personal advantage of these opportunities. *Organize your thinking.*

5. What can you contribute to the boss and the group that will benefit you? After all, everything you do affects your self-interest. You can give your aggressiveness in getting work done, your enterprise in doing it efficiently and imaginatively, your enthusiasm in reaching objectives, and your acceptance of responsibility in doing things right. *Plan your contributions.*

You're almost there.

Smoothing out today's emotional highs and lows

Each day is a variety of wins and losses, good moods and bad moods. All of us want uneventful days when we're left alone to do our thing our own way. Not many of us get days like these. What can you expect of this day in emotional highs and lows? How can you smooth them out?

1. *Your emotional enemies* Moods of various nature can get you down. The emotional enemies you want to avoid include:

- depression
- resentment
- irritation
- anxiety
- perfectionism

- frustration
- intolerance
- envy
- hostility
- guilt

- inadequacy
- resistance
- self-hate
- inferiority
- opposition

2. *Your friendly attitudes* You counteract these emotional enemies by bringing into play the friendly attitudes that conquer negative feelings. These attitudes include:

- exuberance
- humor
- understanding
- respectfulness

- loyalty
- self-stimulation
- unflappability
- flexibility

- compassion
- enthusiasm
- discretion
- imaginativeness

Why be a victim of emotional lows when you can smooth things out with your emotional highs? There is no need to pay the penalty demanded by ugly moods when you can enjoy a better day, a smoother day, by concentrating on your friendly attitudes. Be friendly!

Digging more for yourself out of this business day

Are you making the all too human mistake of thinking that the good things of life are all in the future? *They're here right now.* Look at it this way:

1. You don't owe this day to your boss or organization.
2. You owe it to yourself.
3. It is a day for you to do something for yourself.
4. Your needs come first; your self-interest is first on the list.
5. No one owns you; you're in control of your own life.
6. You'll resist any "message" that you get from the boss, coworkers, or top management that you're some sort of commodity to be manipulated and controlled. You'll retain your own identity.
7. You'll do what you can to improve your lot in life by making yourself a more attractive investment to your boss.
8. You'll enjoy your contributions to the boss, the group, and the organization because you *want* to contribute and to enjoy achievement.

What are the "good things of life"? Success in being yourself. Success in meeting challenges. Success in learning from failure. Success in overcoming fears, anxieties, and other enemy moods. Success in earning more money so that you can have more security, more evidence that you're making it in the business world.

These things are not in the future. *They're here right now.* Today you can work for yourself in digging more of them out of the business world.

Start digging!

Sidestep damaging situations today

Doing well in your job is one thing. Doing badly is another. There are any number of situations that can pop up and damage your forward progress. You've had some of them happen to you on previous days. How about sidestepping them today? Consider this "awareness" list:

1. Mistakes. There's an old saying that it's not wrong to make mistakes, it's wrong to deny they were made. Mistakes offer you a way to learn. Don't deny them; admit them and go on from there.

2. *Failure fear* It's built into us to fear failure. But you will fail from time to time to reach your objectives. If you're doing your job, you'll win many times and lose a few times. Fight the urge to fear failure. Condition yourself to replace this fear with the philosophy that every human fails occasionally. Don't make a mountain out of this pebble.

3. *Inflexibility* When you're inflexible, you seek to avoid exposure of your emotions. Adapt to change, no matter how small or large. Be reasonable with other people's views. Stay loose and objective. You'll be the winner.

4. *Competitiveness* This is fine up to a certain point. That point is reached when you become bitter after comparing yourself with the successes of others, and when you want to discredit or hamper them. You're the loser.

5. *Overreacting* Things don't go your way and you overreact with anger, sharp criticism, defensiveness. This is like hitting yourself on the head with a hammer. Why hurt yourself?

6. *Lack of inquisitiveness* If you don't ask questions, if you don't speak up and get the facts, how can you understand a situation? No one I know of ever got shot by a boss for asking questions. If you want information, get it! It's your job to do so.

7. *Misunderstanding* You can misunderstand almost anything if you lack the facts on which to base a judgment or make a decision. This ties in with inquisitiveness. Find out the facts, and your score of misunderstandings will drop to zero.

8. *Conflict* Making yourself and your position misunderstood can lead to conflicts with your boss and coworkers. Conflict arises when you and the other person don't understand each other. Get busy and *make* yourself understood. Conflicts never help you move forward.

9. *Procrastination* So you want to put off something? Why? Because you are indecisive. This nondecision process allows work to pile up and misunderstandings to grow. If you're troubled by an assignment, don't put it off. Talk to your boss about it. That's action. Action will help you avoid procrastination.

10. Self-punishment Do you carry the worries of the world on your shoulders? No one asked you to. Why punish yourself because you can't accomplish everything in a day's time? Or when someone else goofs because you played a small part in the events leading to that goof? Admit that you're not perfect and that neither is anyone else. Stop punishing yourself or feeling guilty about things that go blooie.

The business world in which you walk is filled with pitfalls and traps like these. Sidestep them and stay on firm ground. Knowing that they exist alerts you and keeps you wary of ensnarement by them.

Watch what you say and do!

What you can accomplish for yourself this day

The work day has been moving right along. You've got a game plan, you're smoothing out emotional highs and lows, you're avoiding damaging situations. What can you accomplish for *you* on this day? Here are some accomplishments to aim for:

1. Digestible work No matter how big the assignment or how heavy the workload, you can break everything down into easily digestible parts. Put your workload down on paper. Assign first, second, and third priorities to the parts. Take on the first group, then the second, then the third. Size can't frighten you when you disassemble work into small pieces.

2. Reporting to your boss Today you'll plan this, rehearse it, and carry it off in clear, concise terms. Your boss will know what you've been doing, where you're making progress, and what's left to be done. Your businesslike attitude makes you shine like a jewel.

3. Solving problems What *is* the problem—what needs to be done? Then you get busy doing what needs to be done. You accept responsibility for clearing up the problem even though you didn't cause it. That's professionalism. *That's progress for you.*

4. Selling your ideas Shrinking violets aren't persuasive. You are. You speak and make yourself heard, calmly, coolly, with ease. Expressing yourself is absolutely essential to your growth.

5. Standing firmly No one will walk over you. No one will humiliate you, crush you. You'll stick up for yourself and your ideas and values.

Lunch time: ask yourself, "What do I believe about business?"

Another quiet, contemplative moment comes at lunch time. The morning has gone by quickly; the afternoon ahead waits. What do you believe about the business world? Do you believe this?

There are vast changes bubbling within the business world. The power structure is subtly changing. Old practices and methods of management are undergoing slow but sure alterations. There is plenty of room for me in the business world, plenty of opportunities. No one can cause me as much trouble as I can cause myself by not having a clear picture of business, how it operates, and where it is going. My success is in my hands, in no one else's. Despite its many shortcomings, and the difficulties of working for a living, I see the business world as an exciting place. I see myself as contributing to the success of my organization. I won't bite the hand that feeds me. I'll do all I can to make it work better.

Do you also believe this? *I will also find ways to develop mutual friendly harmony with my boss because my boss represents my key to the business world.*

Good! Now it's time to get back to work.

The afternoon: stepping up your self-esteem

Develop your total capabilities. That's a fine-sounding statement. What it means includes:

1. *Enthusiasm* When you feel enthusiastic about your boss, your job, and your organization, you're building your self-esteem.

2. Leadership You're working to become an effective leader, first of yourself and second of other people. Today you'll move forward in leadership development.

3. *Ego* This is where you live. When you face the realities of life, adjust to them, and set your sights on constant improvement, you strengthen your ego.

4. *Enterprise* This means you get off your duff and do things, but not in a mechanical, slavish sort of way. You use imagination—look for new ways to do old things. You are creative, refusing to be locked into worthless and meaningless work methods when you see that you can do them in a better, more efficient way.

5. *Personal force* Wrap up ego, self-confidence, and self-image and mix them with a desire to get ahead in the business world, and you have an unbeatable personal force.

Self-esteem is a precious power. When you think well of yourself, your total capabilities improve immensely. This afternoon is an excellent time for building your self-esteem. Work on it!

Setting up a successful business day tomorrow

In a little while you'll be going home. Now is the time to set up the next business day so that you can get off to a good start. Organize your work so that when you return you'll be in control. You'll get off at a fast pace.

Remind yourself:

1. I am accountable for my work. I'll lay it out for tomorrow so that I'll have the least amount of difficulty in getting started.

2. I'll make notes of the things I must communicate to others. I'll handle those communications, leaving nothing undone.

3. As I do these things, I'll be philosophical about the neatness of my plans and how unforeseen problems can pop up at any moment. I'll be mentally prepared to accept the problems and work at solving them. Then I'll return to my programmed workload.

Quitting time, and you're still in charge of your own destiny

You're on your way home. The business day is behind you and you're free to do things for yourself, to have fun, to enjoy life. Anyone who doesn't feel a refreshing sense of freedom, of sudden release, at quitting time just isn't with it. Compulsive workers—workaholics—can remain at their desk or pack work home. Your values are different.

You *have* applied yourself. Your performance during the day was good to excellent. You've *earned* your evening free of any holdover or lingering ties with the job, the boss, and your organization.

Heading home, ask yourself: How creative was I today? How much courage did I display in meeting obstacles? How did I help myself in trying to reach my goals of more money and more recognition?

Looking back is easier than looking ahead. Did your good character traits come to your rescue? Did you apply more self-help than self-hate? Did your incentives to improve yourself end with your learning something new this day?

You're autonomous now, on your own. It's a good time to assess what you accomplished for yourself during the day. You see that the business world isn't all that difficult on a mechanical, routine work basis. *It is people who make the business world difficult.* You've learned again that you move ahead in this world directly in response to how hard you paddle your own canoe.

That wonderful feeling of emotional balance

One of the truly fine feelings you can possess is when things are harmonious between you and your boss, your coworkers, and your family. This situation does exist. Sometimes we're not even aware of how close to it we are, so anxious and concerned are we about trivial things. Being human, we're more likely to center our attention on the negative aspects of life than on our positive assets.

Harmony between you and the others in your world is a splendid thing. Most often harmony such as this exists for spurts, and then the problems of life well up and we're engulfed in small and large battles.

A well-balanced emotional situation is difficult to achieve for long periods of time. Some people have a natural knack for achieving it. Most of us, all by ourselves, manage to tip the scales and we slide into an unbalanced emotional posture.

When things are going well, and you realize that you are enjoying good emotional balance, try to analyze what you have been doing that has set up this precious harmony. You'll find that you, more than the others, have contributed to this blessing. Keep on doing what you're doing, it's working!

And when things get unbalanced, go back to working at restoring the harmony. The more you keep trying, the more chance you have to set things back to where you can enjoy life a great deal more.

It is a splendid feeling, this emotional balance on the job.

After work: what you owe your family and friends

Since you must work in order to survive and pay your way, you adjust yourself to the demanding conditions of the business world. But on your own time, you set your own conditions. These include how well you mesh with your family and friends.

It is a strange feature of many Americans that they accent their job more than they do their own family and friends. They take their job worries home with them, talk about their work constantly, and bore the heck out of everyone. You're smarter: you leave the job where it belongs—waiting for you the next business day.

Give your family full attention. *Listen to them.* Be generous with your time and attention. Do the same with your friends. They're not really so much interested in what happened to *you* that day as in what happened to *them.* Look at this giving of yourself to them as a form of stimulation. It will take your mind off yourself. It will provide you with the refreshing electricity that charges your battery.

It's your life. You enjoy it more on your free time when you share it with those whom you love, admire, and respect. When you listen to your family and friends, you'll be listening to their troubles. But interspersed with all that is the thread that means the most to you. It is the invisible thread that binds you with them, the tie between their interest in you and your gentle concern for them.

By the heaviest proportion, your time with your loved ones is the most important part of any day.

You owe yourself a large measure of excellent health

Too many people ignore their health. They smoke too much, drink too much, eat too much, and get little or no exercise.

Look around you at the office or plant one of these days. How many of your coworkers have been really taking care of themselves? Are they overweight, do they have trouble breathing, are they afflicted with stomach trouble, backaches, headaches?

How about you? You know that regular exercise is one of your greatest assets. Long walks are great. Any of the games, like handball, golf, tennis, and sandlot baseball, are great. So are swimming, biking, and jogging. You'd have to be blind not to see the many newspaper and magazine articles on the subject of health and exercise.

We're a nation of dieters. That's because we're a nation that eats too much in the first place. Control of what you stuff into your mouth is essential to your good health. You know that. Why become a constant dieter when you can eat properly in the first place?

Getting rid of the tension of the work day is easy when you exercise (even that long, brisk walk will do it). You let off steam, anxiety fades from you, you're more relaxed. Your health is also tied in with your ability to *enjoy yourself* after work—movies, plays, music concerts, a pet project at home, an evening playing cards with friends, taking the family on a drive. You have your own free-time pattern. Plunge into it, and don't feel guilty about enjoying it. You've earned it, and it's all yours. Tear into it!

The different roles you act out each day

You can be a *daughter.* "Yes, Mom, I'm up. Yes, Mom, I'll take an umbrella." On the way to work you're a *body snatcher,* looking at the men with appreciative eyes. At the office you're the *perfect secretary.* "Yes, Mr. Humble, I'll get Mr. Zero on the phone right away." At the coffee break you're a *hellion,* titillating the girls with, "Wait 'til I tell you what he did after that!" At lunch you're the *very professional woman.*

At the cocktail hour you're a *movie starlet*. "Come admire me!" On a date with your boyfriend, "I'll be your perfect mate." At home, in bed, as sleep comes to take you, you're a *worrier*, "I need to lose five pounds. I must get more exercise. Maybe I'll use a different eye shadow tomorrow. Did I say the right things to Jim?"

You can be a *husband*. "I'll call the gas company about that bill, honey." A *father*. "What happened to the softball I bought you last week?" A *neighbor*. "Sure, Fred, use the lawnmower anytime you want until yours is fixed." A *subordinate*. "Yes, J.B., I'll get right on it!" A *boss*. "Miss Hyphen, take a letter, please." A *friend*. "A hole in one, no kidding! Let's have lunch on me." A *competitor*. "I don't want that baboon getting the promotion. I want it!" A *body snatcher*. "Did you see the short skirt Snookie is wearing today!" A *learner*. "Look at the junk I have to read in order to do the Gamble assignment!"

Whoever you are, you are a multitude of people within the same skin. It's normal, playing different roles. Who would want to play just one of them all day long?

Come on, admit it. You want to like yourself

The day has nearly ended. Time for bed. All in all, how did you do this day? The main judgment is, how well do you like yourself at day's end?

You, like the rest of us, are in an eternal struggle to learn to like yourself. This feeling is not freely given to you. It has to be earned. *It also has to be recognized.*

For example, one highly talented person told me: "I can do one hundred things right during the day, and one thing wrong. I catch hell for that one lousy thing!" So it is with your judgment of yourself. One lousy thing will dampen your spirits and convince you the day was a mess.

Recognize that you have done very well during the day in all departments. Recognize that one clumsy event does not automatically wipe out the one hundred fine things you accomplished. Why berate yourself for one item when there are one hundred to be pleased with?

This "blame technique" is a mistake many of us make. You don't have to make this mistake any more than we must. It is a quirky part of human nature and an unnecessary one.

Go ahead, like yourself. You've had more successes today than failures. You've made progress. You've used your talents to the best of your ability. You've grown a bit. You're doing well. Take satisfaction in those accomplishments.

Go to bed liking yourself. You'll sleep like a log.

You'll find courage to meet big changes

Any really big change in your life will put a great deal of stress on you. A new job, a new boss, a move to a new location. No matter how many times you've made changes before, each new biggie will make you uptight unless you fall back on your courage savings account. Here's how you make the account pay interest for you:

- Remind yourself how normal it is to feel anxiety and the resulting stress where your body reacts psychosomatically.
- Take your time and give yourself a chance to adjust to the new situation.
- Don't rush headlong into a lot of activity. Think things out as calmly as you can at home and try to see what's ahead and how you should prepare yourself to accommodate the change.
- Find someone who has made a change of the same type and ask what the problems were and how that person solved them.
- Remember that all big changes carry a certain amount of frustration, and be prepared to accept a bit of discomfort and strangeness until things settle down.

- Remember that in your lifetime you've met and bested many big changes and that you have the courage and character resources to handle this particular change.
- Reassure yourself that life will go on and that the change will work out to the better for you.

After all, how do you get anywhere in life without accommodating big and little changes? You've the courage, use it.

The tremendous power of common courtesy

Intelligent viewers of our American way of life have noted for many years the inescapable fact that we have become less friendly to each other. They blame TV in part because it keeps people in their homes, giving them rapid accounts of the news and a wide variety of entertainment. Because of this, they reason, many Americans feel less of a *need* for the stimulating company or the good opinion of other people.

I can't quarrel with that. We *have* been drawn apart in this country, not only by the persuasive and magnetic TV presence, but by abrasive racial, sexist, political, and economic forces. Our lives *have* been speeded up, made vastly more complicated, by domestic and international crises. We seem to have become crisis-oriented, even crisis-prone.

In this atmosphere we have become more withdrawn individually, more totally concerned with our own interest, and less inclined to extend old-fashioned common courtesy to others. "Common courtesy" is a term that has been around for a long time. It means that people willingly exchange normal courtesies with each other even if they do not know each other intimately. In short, it means you do not have to have a *reason* to be courteous to someone. You just are.

For *you* there is a tremendous power in common courtesy. When you are courteous to *everyone*, whites, blacks, latinos, the elderly, the young, men and women alike, foreign visitors, anyone you meet, *you are the winner.* You win for these reasons:

1. Everyone responds to courtesy. The few who don't show it *feel it* nevertheless. In their eyes you become a more substantial person. You have established *your presence* with them, and a more friendly atmosphere prevails. You gain not only their attention but their goodwill. Their cooperation can assist you in many ways.

2. You respond to your own courtesy. That's right. You lessen your fear of strangers and even of people whom you know quite well. You lessen your hostility toward people in general, and in its place you feel a strong common bond. This common bond is a powerful force for you. You feel less set apart from the others and more a *significant and worthy part* of the human race.

Ask yourself these questions:

1. How truly courteous have I been lately to everyone I meet?

2. Why haven't I made the effort to be more courteous?

3. What am I losing by not extending common courtesy *to my boss,* the people I work with, the strangers I meet?

4. What effective power can I develop by being courteous?

I don't have to tell you the *ways* in which you can be courteous to your boss and others. You already know. It is your decision to make about using common courtesy.

When *you* make courtesy an integral part of your life style, you find that you stop waiting for others to be courteous to you first. You initiate it and you profit from it. You profit because more people will like and respect you, and you will like and respect yourself even more.

These positive thoughts
help you every work day

A fundamental law of human life is that you must try to balance negative thoughts with positive thoughts. Sometimes this is easier said than done. It's never a snap working at any job, and it's easy to become depressed and uneasy from reading the newspapers and listening to the woes of your friends and relatives. What sort of positive thoughts will help you every work day and balance out the glumness that may inhibit you from making a bit of progress? Try these, which you've learned from this chapter:

- I have a solid idea of who I am, and I feel strongly that I am worthy of success in the business world.
- I am in control of my life, and I know where I am on this particular day of my life.
- I have a well-thought-out plan for my life, and I know where I want to go both in the business world and in my private life.
- I expect to be more successful; I won't settle for less.
- I intend to do what is natural for me and not to accept a job which demeans me, holds me back, or prevents me from achieving what I need out of life.
- I am unique; there is no one else exactly like me.
- I accept responsibility.
- I look for opportunities to move ahead and show my talents.
- I am constantly developing my capabilities and improving myself to do consistently better work.
- I am an active person, involved in my job, my family, my community and delighted to be alive and contributing.
- I will take risks to get ahead.
- I will stay flexible, knowing everything won't work my way all the time.
- I know that I will have tough problems and feel the effects of stress because of the demands on me.
- I will remain enthusiastic about my job and my chances to move ahead in spite of problems and stress.
- I know that when things go wrong I can work to turn a disadvantage into an advantage for me if I stay calm and do the necessary thinking.

- I know there are many differences between people, and I accept this.
- I will work to find innovative ways to cope with conflicts—most importantly, to keep conflicts from cropping up unnecessarily.
- I will offer ideas and suggestions whenever I feel they will help individuals or my boss.
- I will learn to delegate authority, knowing that trying to do everything by myself can lead to trouble.
- I will not maintain a hard personal position about decisions, because I realize there are always several right ways to handle a particular problem.
- I will do something each day for someone else.
- I will get my work done by doing one thing at a time.
- I will prevent anger from gripping me by finding a way to work it off, walk it off, talk it off.
- I will back away from very stressful situations by getting a good night's sleep, taking a short vacation, or spending a relaxing day somewhere away from the problem.
- I know that if I learned poor habits, I can unlearn them with the proper effort.
- I will avoid getting in over my head in areas of responsibility where I'm not fully qualified to operate.
- I know that from time to time I must reexamine my mental outlook, study my emotional reactions to the job and my boss, and determine whether my goals are realistic.
- I know that one of my biggest problems is adapting to this world's fast-changing pace and all of the stresses and tensions these changes create for me.
- I know that success is relative, that it is what *I* believe it to be and not what others say it is.
- I know that I can get what I want out of the business world as long as my objectives are within my capabilities.
- I know that if this day goes blooie, there is always tomorrow.

- I will keep my sense of humor.
- I will use common courtesy with everyone I meet.

This has been a long list of positive thoughts. There are many more, but read this list over from time to time and you'll see that you *are* reinforced in your positive position about life, your job, and your boss.

You help yourself fit more snugly into the business world every time you reinforce your positive position. You fit loosely every time you fall into negative thinking.

6

Developing Winning Ways with an Insensitive Boss

You drew a tough one, an insensitive boss. This person represents one of the most difficult challenges you can face. The insensitivity stems from the boss's fear of other people, including you, and an unconscious desire not to become involved with anyone for fear of getting hurt. This boss overcompensates.

This person comes on as if he or she were the only boss in the world with any brains, with any capability, with any power to decide what is right and what is wrong. This boss has developed some jim-dandy techniques for setting subordinates' teeth on edge. Trying to cope with such a boss as you would with a normal person brings you nothing but dismay, depression, and hostility.

In spite of an abrasive nature, this boss can be mined for whatever amount of friendship he or she is capable of giving you. In fact, some of the most insensitive bosses can be made to flip-flop so well that they become almost gracious in opening doors of fine new opportunities for you.

Not that it is ever easy. I said it was a difficult challenge. You have two choices: to remain in place and take this boss's nonsense, which means you go nowhere, or to do something about it and get somewhere.

This chapter will show you some of the background of why a boss is insensitive and what you can do to succeed with this individual's unwilling or willing help.

What's the very worst thing that can happen?

There is your insensitive boss. And there you are with something you fear might make the boss react against you. You assess your options. Shut up, play it safe, and hate yourself. Speak up and have an argument on your hands.

Your past experiences with your boss have impressed you. You know the boss will react—perhaps mildly, perhaps strongly. Should you bring up the unpleasant subject and your advice about what should be done and take a chance?

What's the very worst thing that can happen? The boss:

1. Flares up and fires you. You go and get a better job.

2. Launches a tirade and later transfers you. You end up with a better boss.

3. Reacts coldly and puts you in the deep freeze. You wait for the boss's guilty feeling to eventually thaw loose and for amends to be made reluctantly.

4. Irritably downgrades you on reports. You find a way to show the boss's boss that you were right.

5. Humiliates you in front of other people. Your boss lost the game right there; you're a hero in their eyes because they know the boss as well as you do.

What are the good things that can happen? The boss:

1. Listens to you about the unpleasant subject but doesn't ac-

cept your advice. The boss *did* listen, and later your advice will be something the boss "just thought of." You win because your solution *was* used.

2. Listens to you and winces about the unpleasant subject but accepts your advice glumly and in poor grace. You're still alive.

3. Is unhappy about the unpleasant subject but agrees with you about what should be done but does nothing. You're breathing.

4. Amazingly accepts the news about the unpleasant subject and asks you to help clear up the problem right away. You've won cleanly! You were honest enough and clear-thinking enough to be persuasive in presenting the troublesome subject and your views about what could be done to straighten things out.

We're our own worst enemy when it comes to toting bad news into the insensitive boss. We fear that the boss's reaction will be against us, the bearer of the bad news, and not against the bad news itself. Give the insensitive boss a chance. If such a boss reacts against *you,* take it in stride.

Most insensitive bosses will come out of their dither later on and secretly respect you for being candid and forthright and for also bringing in some ideas for the solution. The worst thing that can happen isn't that the insensitive boss will get uptight again. The worst thing that can happen is that you will continue to sell yourself short.

Mine! This little empire belongs only to me!

Many insensitive bosses are fond of saying, "I'm not here to build an empire." The translation of that is, "I'm here to build an empire."

Listen to the telltale phrases. A boss of this type will often say "my people," "my department," "my assistant." He will preface quite a few remarks by saying, "My staff is working on my plan."

It is difficult for such a boss to forego the pleasure of identifying everything as personal property. A secretary is "my girl." A male subordinate is "my man." Anything that clears through this boss is "my program."

Building an empire, which means getting as many people as possible reporting directly, is essential to many an insensitive boss's good mental health. It tends to overload payrolls but it does please the empire builder. This boss can look at "my group" and feel that, with so many people reporting directly, he or she must, indeed, be important. The boss is, by that fact, essential. How would everything function if this boss were not there to direct "my people"?

Bosses with this handicap are very insecure people. They salve their anxiety by the numbers game and by unnecessary possessiveness. Trying to get them to cut their staffs is like asking them to cut off an arm or a leg.

An insensitive boss of this type is out for pure self-interest. You mean little to this callous person.

The boss can never crush imaginative Henry

On his way to work Henry invariably found himself thinking of Mr. Baskin, his boss. He didn't like Mr. Baskin and was secretly afraid of him. At the beginning, when he first went to work for the company, he would tremble whenever he had to enter Mr. Baskin's office. The boss was crusty, pompous, often harsh, seldom pleasant. He was a petty tyrant from the old school of bosses.

Henry worked out a simple defense mechanism something along the lines of James Thurber's famous *Secret Life of Walter Mitty*. Whenever he found himself in Mr. Baskin's office, he would imagine he was the Good Guy and the boss was the Bad Guy.

Henry would be the Most Famous Swordsman in France, swishing his blade through the air so that Mr. Baskin's belt would be sliced and, when the boss rose, he imagined Mr. Baskin's pants would fall to the floor. Or, Henry would be a gunfighter, drawing smoothly and shooting a tuft of hair from the side of the boss's balding head.

One day when Mr. Baskin was raising hell about a trivial matter that barely concerned Henry, Henry was unperturbed and smiling. He blunted the boss's corrosive monologue as he had learned he could do by remaining calm and unflappable. It was easy for Henry. He was a Pirate Captain, and in his mind he was making Mr. Baskin walk the plank!

Going into a whimpering fit whenever an insensitive boss snarls at you is self-defeating. Henry had learned that lesson. He protected his thin ego by fantasies.

An indifferent, ego-killing boss is a terrible menace to put up with. If you have the imagination that Henry had, you can use his method. Whatever you do, protect your ego. Keep it healthy and unscarred, no matter how disturbing your flint-hearted boss may be.

Bosses of this type seldom set out to destroy egos. What they are seeking to demonstrate usually is the old boss-crutch emotion, "Don't you feel sorry for me, putting up with the terrible incompetency around here? How I suffer!"

Look who's incompetent!

How to duck under your boss's left hook

There are all kinds of sparring between you and your insensitive male boss. It can take place one-on-one when you're in the boss's office, or in memos and directives, or in meetings. It has an effect on you if you don't know how to duck.

The boss's left hook is whatever characteristic gesture is used to say in effect, "Damn it, I'm running this show, and what I say goes!" You can take the punch and signal that you understood. "Yes, master." You shiver in frustration. You can block the punch by standing there with only a meek hand upraised and say, "Don't you want our views and suggestions?" You feel the phantom blow and it hurts.

Learning to duck under the boss's left hook isn't so difficult. When the boss is on you, for whatever reason, your shoulders will rise, just like a boxer's. You'll clench your fists. You'll pull your head down. You're under some form of attack, and the climate is a bit combative, a bit hostile.

If the boss is right and you're wrong, you feel guilty—and who likes that feeling? If you're right and the boss is wrong, you feel powerless to give it back as hard as you're getting it—and no one likes that feeling, either.

Regardless of how totally unnecessary the donnybrook that got started between you and your boss—whether it's a reasonable demand on your boss's part or a crass act of injustice—you owe yourself something right away.

The art of ducking. And you can do it sitting or standing. It's simple. *Make your shoulders go down!*

Once you remove yourself from a strike-back position, you remove yourself from a stance where you can be hit and hurt. You're more able to think clearly, to say the appropriate things, and to assume the appropriate facial and body expressions.

With your shoulders down, *you are in command of you.* Your boss is not able to provoke you, disturb you, or rile you. Few bosses realize the effect they have on people they are bawling out, or criticizing or "making sense to." All they see is that they have a problem, and they're "calling it to your attention."

They're still swinging left hooks, no matter what pains they go to to cover it up with words. Your job is not to let it have a serious effect on you. It is part of the business world's hall of ancient tortures.

When you find yourself in such a situation, fall back immediately to the safest posture of all—*shoulders down!* Listen to your boss—not only *what* is said, but *how* it is said. Your boss will reveal what is really bothering him or her. Perhaps someone else goofed and it's being taken out on you. Perhaps your boss goofed and is looking for a scapegoat. Perhaps you botched up an assignment and your boss has got you cold.

Tick off these thoughts in your mind quickly:

1. What really is the situation?
2. Who is the boss really sore at?
3. What part did I play in this mess?
4. What needs to be done to straighten things out?
5. What does the boss want to hear from me?
6. What is the most political thing I can say right now?

With your shoulders down, you're ready to reason and persuade, not fight. Fighting will get you a free trip through the tunnel to nowhere.

After all, a problem does exist, even if it is only in the mind of your troublemaker boss. As far as your boss is concerned, it's a serious problem. Your job is to help find ways to solve that problem, right now.

If you find yourself in this unpleasant situation, go through the simple checklist of thoughts above. And keep your shoulders down and relaxed. You'll be able to function effectively and turn that moment into an achievement for you.

How to give your boss
an overdue comeuppance

Attractive as it is, punching your insensitive male boss in the mouth is a definite no-no regardless of how abrasive and abusive the boss may be. Your pleasure will be short-term. You'll either get punched back (rarely, since bosses aren't usually courageous fighters), fired, blacklisted, sued, demoted, or put in the corporate deep-freeze by being transferred to whatever serves as Siberia.

We all fantasize about giving the boss an overdue comeuppance. Rearranging the boss's nose is the worst way to do it. In fact, you'll thereby create sympathy for your boss. You may be a secret hero to some of your coworkers, who will never back you up in public, but you've created a bad scene for yourself from which you may never recover. So why bother?

There are other ways. None of them are foolproof and I don't recommend any of them. I mention them only because I understand that they have been used by other people who have chafed and sweated under unusually mean bosses and found a way or two to strike back without getting tossed into the penalty box.

Harry was in charge of audio-visuals for a large food product company. Harry was irritated mostly by his advertising-manager boss for several reasons: the boss had passed over Harry for a merit pay raise; he held senseless, time-wasting meetings; and he swore copiously in what appeared to be a subconscious effort to stress his masculinity.

Pondering what he could do to whack his boss without getting caught, Harry had an idea. Into each meeting he carried a tiny tape recorder hidden in his pants pocket. The corded microphone was hidden behind his tie. In a few months he was able to make a composite tape of the boss's voice in a ten-minute outpouring of dirty language, shouting, table pounding, and tasteless ethnic jokes. Harry had copies made in a nearby city and then mailed them anonymously to the president of the company, the boss's wife, and the president of the boss's golf club. What carried the authority for the tape was that the boss had a very strong, gravelly distinctive type of voice.

In a matter of days, the boss ceased calling meetings, kept out of sight, and in a few months had obtained a job with another company. Harry never knew whether his former boss suspected him nor did he feel guilty about giving his boss a long-due comeuppance.

Mildred couldn't find it in her heart to like her new boss, Cliff, in the traffic department. She knew that he had cruelly and mercilessly undermined her previous boss to such an extent that he, Cliff, was able to get the older man's job. Mildred felt that it was just a matter of time before she, too, would be eased out by the new back-stabber.

Mildred was a coward. She couldn't face Cliff and tell him to his face how she felt, because she didn't want to risk the twenty-three years she had in the pension fund. She didn't want to leave and find another job. She developed a cowardly approach. She could, through friends in the controller's office, obtain Xerox copies of Cliff's expense accounts. After all, with twenty-three years with the company, she had *some* friends.

She pored over the expense sheets, finding dozens of instances of cheating, liberty-taking, and free-swinging. She knew her boss's superior was the kind who wouldn't bother personally checking reports, so on each sheet she neatly lettered the company regulation that had been bent, twisted, or snapped. When she had a large enough stack, she had only to wait until Cliff was on a three-day trip out of town. She routed the stack in an intercompany envelope to the boss's superior. Again, anonymously.

When her boss returned, he had an ugly session explaining the expense reports. Cliff kept his job, but he was obviously a subdued man. It was all Mildred could do to keep a straight face whenever she had to deal directly with the vastly chastened back-stabber.

Terry had a different approach. His boss, Norman, was not only abrasive, he was absolutely inept at delegating authority and keeping work on schedule in a large office of a national trade association. Terry's efforts to work with his boss met with rejection after rejection, doused with the boss's watering-down of purpose and aim and with his ineptness at understanding and decision-making.

Terry worked out a program on paper that had everything that should be done, goals, a time schedule, and a step-by-step procedure for the department. He took his case to his co-workers. So persuasive was he and so in agreement were they that he was able to march nine of them into Norman's office and present the program to the astonished man.

The men refused to sit and remained standing while the boss read the document, his face growing a dark red. Terry was able to deliver the ultimatum. If Norman didn't accept the program and put it into work immediately, the group was going to take their grievance to the executive secretary of the association.

It took some doing, some loud and angry talking, but Terry and his coworkers won. Norman became less abrasive and began to listen more. While the situation never became a bed of roses, it did improve. Word of Terry's action reached higher quarters. Within a year a new post had been created for him. He is still with the association and is in line to be the executive secretary one day.

These people were driven to strong measures in their efforts to combat insensitive bosses. They proved, *as you can*, that people with some courage and imagination can give it back as hard as it is dished out. Unfeeling, cold, and detached bosses can be given their long-overdue comeuppance.

Is your boss making you fat?

Some recent studies have shown that many people overeat because of their great unhappiness with themselves. It is entirely possible that many a boss who is difficult to work with may be the culprit in making people fat.

The simple frustration of not being able to "tell off" the unresponsive boss, of not being able to correct a serious mistake the boss has made, of not being a part of the decision-making team, can bring unhappiness to anyone.

Some employees deal with this unhappiness by having one or

more cocktails at lunch and dinner time. Some are in danger of getting, or already have, ulcers, colitis, or some other emotion-originated body breakdown.

Your boss can be making you fat by causing more stress than you can cope with. You deal with this stress by overeating. If you have been putting on weight, ask yourself these questions:

1. Do I get to thinking about the boss at home and then head for the refrigerator or pantry to get something to eat?

2. Do I keep candy or other goodies in my desk to eat after I've had a meeting with the boss?

3. Do I head for a cocktail bar after work to have a pickup because I'm still uneasy about the boss?

4. Is food becoming a tranquilizer for me, so that when I eat a big snack before I go to bed I sleep better and worry less about the boss?

Your honest answers will tell you whether your boss is the culprit in making you put on extra weight. Why permit this?

Your boss can make you physically fit

Why not? Instead of taking the troubles of the day home with you inside a churning stomach, a seething mind, and a rigid body that won't let you go to sleep at bedtime, try turning this energy into something to benefit you.

Your difficulty is energy. But it is energy spent inward, creating physical and mental troubles for you. Use this energy to exercise. Long walks done briskly are great. They can be done almost anytime, and they do the best good when you start them about twenty minutes after your evening meal.

Depending on the weather and season, there are things like tennis, golf, swimming, rowing, skiing, and skating—all kinds of attractive sports. In the privacy of your home or apartment you can do the types of calisthenics that appeal to you. Running in place for five or ten minutes in the morning and evening will do wonders for anyone.

The trick is to get your frustrations *out* of yourself. Keep them boxed inside and you face problems, even a heart attack. Get them out and put this energy to work building and maintaining a more healthy body.

You're the winner if you do. Why let your insensitive boss or the problems at the office or plant bug you? Start now, no matter how trivial the exercise, and keep it up. You'll see what I mean.

Have you been avoiding your flint-hearted boss lately?

There are few truly flint-hearted bosses in the business world. It may be your poor fortune to have one of the few. Have you found that you've been going out of your way to avoid this creature who is a throwback to the gent who foreclosed on Little Nell's mortgage?

Avoiding a boss is not an unusual occurrence. It is natural to want to spend time with a friendly boss, because the experience is rewarding. An insensitive boss is something else; who wants to be subjected to the cold aloofness of this person?

When you begin to avoid this type of boss, you're sending up a distress signal. You're frustrated. You're hiding from even a small confrontation with this boss because you fear some damage to your ego, another putdown, another feeling of not being accepted, another feeling of losing dignity. You fear speaking up because of what this boss might do to retaliate.

This boss might already have a history of retaliations that you've either seen or heard of. Again, do you want to give in to a fear, or a deep anxiety, or do you want to do something to place yourself in a better position? Let's assume your boss is a man. Consider this course of action:

1. Seek an appointment with him. Have your thoughts well organized. Try a frontal assault. Say something like, "I'm puzzled why I find it harder and harder to come and see you. This is bad because it's inhibiting me from serving effectively under you."

2. Flintheart will be amazed. This boss is convinced, of course, that he's a perfect business machine, admired by everyone, and that all in the group should be delighted to be working with such a winner. He'll wonder what the problem is.

This is the starter. If you don't heap complaint after complaint on him, but just act puzzled as to *why* you feel inhibited, there is a chance that he can come to see that he hasn't been treating you or the others very well. A chance, I said. Flinthearts are not always flip-flops. I'm gambling that you will, at least, see *some* improvements in your relations with him.

A frontal assault is not easy, whether your boss is male or female. It takes courage. You can lose as well as win. But try it. If it works, you're better off. If it doesn't, start looking around. Life is too short for you to be working under corrosive conditions where you spend time avoiding your boss.

When your boss is on the wrong track

Arthur became alarmed in the course of a meeting when he saw that his boss was on a wrong track. His boss was a chilly person, stiff-backed, with no talent for give-and-take in a meeting. He was heavy-handed, boring others with windy rambling that went afar from the subjects on the agenda.

Arthur fought back the strong temptation to say, "That's silly!" The boss wanted to purchase some expensive duplicating equipment that Arthur knew, from first-hand experience, was not what the group needed. The purchase would eat into their budget and they'd have a costly white elephant taking up space.

Instead, Arthur was patient. An admirable quality. In the meeting he forced the conversation to other areas and by ending time the purchase had been postponed until the next meeting a week away. Each day, Arthur sought out the boss and bit by bit began to paint the true picture of the equipment the boss wanted to buy. "I know how interested you are in evaluating it," he said, "and I have these reports from outside sources that will give you more facts." Arthur gave the boss the negative reports he'd dug up to prove his point.

When the next meeting came around, the question of the new equipment was not on the agenda, nor did the boss say anything about it. The boss never said "Thank you" to him, but Arthur knew from experience that he had again kept his boss from going down a wrong path.

Patience and timing. They work wonders when you're dealing with a boss of this type.

Your boss doesn't make you a slave—you do

An unfeeling boss cannot enslave you. Your life can be made more difficult because this boss is a frosty individual who is not concerned with your welfare and self-interest. But in no way can any boss force you to stay there and take remote indifference and studied callousness month after month, year after year.

I've personally met very few really unfeeling bosses. I know they exist and that there will always be some men and women in bossdom who fit this description. The point isn't whether they'll last long where they are, or whether they'll go higher. The point is that while they are bosses, they can be very difficult persons to work with.

You do not have to stay and work with a distant, unfeeling boss. If you stay, you're the one who is enslaving you, not your boss. You stay, not because you're afraid that if you go out and get another job you may end up with another boss of the same type. You stay because *the thought of a change is more unnerving to you than the thought of staying.* You lack enough get-up-and-go to move along. You might have a vain hope that "things will improve."

We're all victims in one way or another of these ridiculous fears. We fear a boss because that person can fire us, make our lives miserable, create unhappy climates in which we must work, fail to give us merit pay raises, and so forth.

Sometimes we turn our frustration on ourselves, cutting our good opinion of ourself by becoming very critical of our actions and station in life. We have allowed the boss to turn our fears into a form of self-attack where we become seriously injured emotionally. This sort of thing is ridiculous!

If you can't work things out by a frontal assault on an insensitive boss, or by patiently trying to swing the boss around to a more human way of working with you, then get out. Don't be a slave. It is never the boss who is keeping you there, it is you.

You're in control of your own life. Make your own decisions, plan what you want to do, then do it. Your biggest threat is that if you stay with an insensitive boss for a long time, *you* might end up becoming just as insensitive to others yourself.

Fear is what makes a boss insensitive

We've been talking about an "insensitive" boss, and it's time to take a look at *why* this type of boss is insensitive to your human needs. There are several broad conclusions:

1. The largest percentage of bosses *are not trained properly to function effectively as managers of other people.*

2. Many bosses are promoted upward on their individual ability to get things done, *and not always on their ability to work well with other people.* They often are promoted above

their level of competency. They were great as individuals but they poop out as leaders.

3. The *aggressive traits* many of these bosses have that made them successes as individuals often work against them when they are put in charge of other people.

4. Once an insecure individual has been put in charge of other people, *it is fear that makes that boss insensitive to the needs of the people below.*

I said these are broad conclusions. They don't apply to every insensitive boss, but they do to most of them. The most basic *why* of their insensitivity is *fear.*

Remember this about bosses. Once they have been promoted to a boss spot, they have more to win and more to lose. They don't want to do anything that would make them lose what they have won or jeopardize what they might win in the future.

On the previous pages we looked at some examples of insensitive bosses and people's reactions to them. Let's see if we can't put together a composite picture of the "average insensitive boss" who is controlled more by *hidden fears* than by a well-developed sense of human relations. The average insensitive boss is fear-prompted to:

1. Avoid being revealed as uncertain, foolish, unknowledgeable, or lacking in skills or talents.

2. Avoid being subjected to criticism or having decisions and judgments questioned.

3. Sidestep questions that this boss can't answer correctly.

4. Keep everyone out of the decision-making process.

5. Escape exposure to different points of view that clash with the boss's.

6. Avoid communicating to the group in an effort to prevent fancied "reaction" from the more alert ones.

7. Keep information from the group in the belief that things are better if the employees are not kept informed.

8. Take all of the credit for the group's work in an effort to impress the boss's boss.

9. Control everything in the staunch belief that he or she is indispensable in making things run.

10. "Protect the territory," in the belief that this boss "owns" the job and the people involved in it.

The average insensitive boss has no loyalty to anyone who reports to him or her, doesn't like getting close to them, savors authority, and doesn't want it challenged in even the smallest way. This boss enjoys the tribal rituals of being a boss where chieftains are bowed to and the lowly "keep their place."

This boss lacks poise and maturity, is too sensitive to cope easily with others, can't stand face-to-face confrontations, and enjoys belittling or undercutting those in the group.

Because this boss is disturbed by deep anxieties, he or she is extremely uneasy about holding the boss job. This person is given to intense jealousy and resents others who have talent and good capabilities. This person is fearful of newcomers who might shine brightly and move in on the boss's job and of those longer-term people in the group who do outstanding work.

The average insensitive boss finds it difficult to help others, hears only what he or she wants to hear, isolates those who might be a threat to the boss job, and fails deliberately to develop a successor to that job. In short, this boss is turned off in connection with other people and is concerned most with protecting territory and authority. Usually, this is done by means of small, petty, cheap, and totally unnecessary activities designed to demean, deflate, and dehumanize others.

You, working with this type of boss, are left to speculate *how* the average insensitive boss came to be such an inadequate, selfish, fearful person. The answer lies in the childhood and growing-up process of this boss. Some disastrous emotional events have happened—of that you can be certain.

These emotional upheavals created a deep inner fear of failure, a self-distrust, and a feeling of self-unworthiness in comparison with others. This boss has a compelling inner drive to succeed, to *prove* that he or she has some value in the world.

But, and this is the critical point, this boss rarely feels the need to be fully considerate of other people. Others are seen, not as individuals with their own human rights, but as tools to be used in that tangled, fearful, desperate drive to succeed.

You can't mend the damage that has been done to this type of boss. You can only minimize the effect the insensitivity has on you by *understanding* the why of the problems this boss creates for you and the others. This isn't easy. Read on and see how you might win in spite of the difficulties of having such an "average insensitive boss."

Working your winning ways with an insensitive boss

If you see good opportunities for you in your present organization, it well may be worth your time and effort to stay and work your winning ways on the major roadblock to those opportunities, your insensitive boss. This has been done successfully by countless others and it can be done successfully by you. Follow these guidelines:

1. You don't blow your cool, no matter how abrasive the boss becomes. You condition yourself to remain unflappable because *you know in advance* that the boss is capable of setting up corrosive situations. You're prepared because you expect it.

2. You think of who the winner will be if you *are* persistent in carrying out your plans to move ahead. You win first and the boss wins second. The strained-human-relations condition between you and this boss can be overcome if you do your work especially well and avoid total combat with this person.

3. While avoiding direct combat, you don't avoid sticking up for yourself in as forthright and calm a manner as possible. You don't have to take a lot of guff from this boss, and you can say so. Just don't light any fuses when you're saying so! Don't be goaded into an outright fight that only this boss can win.

4. As difficult as it may be to accept, don't think of your

problems with this insensitive boss as *personal*. This type of boss afflicts everyone, not just you, with the viruses of discontent and anxiety. Think of this boss in the abstract. Try not to see it all on a one-to-one basis.

As long as you feel there are genuine opportunities ahead in this organization, your job is to get past the insensitive boss and on to better things. Follow these guidelines and others of your natural instincts, and you'll make it.

7

Helping a Truly Responsive Boss Move You Upward

You lucked out. You drew a good boss, one who is responsive to others and who cares about working well with them and helping them move upward. There are far more bosses of this type than of the insensitive kind.

How do *you* help your responsive boss help you up the ladder? That's what this chapter is all about. As it is in all other matters affecting your life, you are in charge of yourself. It is *your* responsibility, not your boss's, to get somewhere meaningful in the business world.

Your responsibility is to work with your boss, to help the boss wherever possible, in the right manner—to put your efforts into assisting the boss to achieve the goals that have been set forth for your group. Your job is easier in the sense that you have someone friendly to work *with*. It is easier because you have better rapport, better mutual understanding, and the opportunity to "talk things out," and you receive reassuring signals that you are making progress.

You can't take deliberate advantage of a good boss. You can't say, slyly, "The boss is easy. I'll coast. I won't have to work as hard." This is nonsense. You have to work just as hard with a good boss as with a bad one to make progress for yourself.

The pages ahead will give you some solid ideas of how you can go about establishing effective harmony with your boss when your boss is clearly friendly and helpful to you.

A portrait of a really good boss

You're ahead of me. You already know many of the qualities a good boss possesses. Let's look at this checklist, anyway, and measure your boss against it. *A really good boss:*

1. *Makes you feel important in the scheme of things.*

2. *Never criticizes you in front of others.*

3. *Compliments you on your good work.*

4. *Takes pains to show you how to do something better when you make a mistake.*

5. *Keeps you informed of what's going on.*

6. *Asks your advice on certain matters where you have expertise.*

7. *Listens to you when you talk.*

8. *Responds to you frankly and openly when you ask questions.*

9. *Treats the others in the group the same way—doesn't play favorites.*

10. *Doesn't want sycophants, pets, or toadies around.*

11. *Sticks up for you when it is necessary and doesn't have to be asked to do so.*

12. *Talks to you annually about the progress you're making, asks where you need help, and gives you the merit raises you've earned.*

That's some boss.

Your boss can appreciate you

You never appreciate yourself the way other people do. The reason is simple. You see yourself from a limited vantage point. You're too much aware of your shortcomings and not sufficiently impressed with your "longcomings."

You know you've done a lot of things well and that you should be proud of them. This feeling is watered down by your vivid memories of the few times when you didn't come out a winner, when you flopped, bombed out, screwed up, drew a goose egg. Like the rest of us, you're more impressed with your blemishes.

Your good boss knows you far better than you realize. Your boss is in an excellent position to evaluate both your work and you as an individual and to do this objectively. Your blemishes aren't important; your good features are.

Scotty had a good boss and knew it. But Scotty's opinion of himself was low. He lacked courage and conviction. While his work was satisfactory, his long-time feeling that he would never amount to anything kept him from striking out for better things.

Scotty's boss encouraged him to take nighttime courses at a downtown center to pick up some additional skills. Scotty completed them with good grades. The boss suggested, casually, that Scotty get into a speech instruction course. Scotty did, and learned, to his surprise, after a few months, that he had a voice and wouldn't die when he was up before a group.

The boss complimented Scotty whenever Scotty wore an attractive tie. Scotty responded by buying new clothes. He liked the idea of being complimented on dressing well. The boss put him in charge of a string of small committees with well-defined objectives. Scotty came along beautifully in conducting the committee work.

When Scotty won a promotion, it didn't occur to him who had won the promotion. He thought he had. He was wrong. His good, responsive, thoughtful, far-thinking boss had won. The boss had helped turn Scotty from a hold-back guy to a go-ahead guy.

Your good boss can appreciate you. When you respond to the appreciation of your finer points, you move ahead. You even learn to appreciate yourself more.

Your good boss knows you far better than you realize (deliberate repeat). Rely on that high opinion and chase away any lower opinion of yourself that you may have been holding.

Why your good boss wants to help you

When you show that you want to get ahead, your good boss will respond. Developing people in the group is part of a boss's responsibility. All good bosses had some help getting where they are. They remember how pleasant it was to have had a helping hand extended to them now and then.

Your boss will help you for some or all of these reasons:

1. A desire to increase the total competency of the group.

2. A firm conviction that it is better to "grow" a person already on the staff than to search around for a replacement who will require a period of settling down and extra time and effort in training.

3. A responsiveness to your desire, which you've indicated by your efforts to do a consistently better job, to put your talents to increasingly more effective use.

4. A feeling of satisfaction that helping you is helping the company and the business world in general by stepping up your competence level.

5. A desire to fill a need in the group for assistance in a newly opened area by starting fresh with someone who can be trusted to take on the new responsibility.

If the boss wants to help you, shouldn't you make it more attractive for the boss to do so? When you buckle down and take your work seriously, when you show the boss that you want to move ahead, you make it easier for the boss to help you win more of the things you want out of the business world.

Does your boss ever admit to being wrong?

How many times have you heard your boss admit being wrong? How many times have you admitted that you were wrong? It is part of the human way for us *not* to want to openly admit that we goofed, pulled a boner, messed up things, made a mistake, misunderstood the situation, botched an assignment.

If your boss has made such an admission, then your boss is a fine person. If you have made similar admissions, then you're on the same right track. The lesson you learn from admitting a mistake is that humans are mistake-makers. When a mistake is made and openly admitted to, it is far easier to prevent that same mistake from being made again.

The next time your boss says, "Well, I sure did a lousy job on that," give the boss credit. The sin isn't in making a mistake but in denying that one was made. No corporation profits from mistakes that are covered up. Corporations profit from mistakes that are not made time and time again.

Constructive criticism or "being picked on"?

Janet dreaded criticism. As a member of the traffic department of a large advertising agency, it was her job to ride herd on advertisements moving from the art, copy, and production departments. She made mistakes now and then, and when her good boss talked to her in an effort to prevent the mistakes from cropping up again, she resented what she felt was undue criticism.

Janet felt she was "being picked on." She brooded about this fancied injustice and finally went to the vice president who had the traffic department responsibility. She said she would quit if her boss didn't stop picking on her. The other girls made mistakes, and she'd never heard of *them* being called down for it.

The vice president called the boss in, and the three of them had a chat. The boss was ready. This is what her boss said: "Janet, when I've talked to you about your mistakes, it has been in my office where no one could hear us. Some of your mistakes have resulted in our getting into serious trouble with three of our best clients. All I've asked you to do is go by the book, do exactly what has to be done and on time, so that our department isn't guilty of getting the agency in trouble by losing good clients. I've done the same things with the other girls you mentioned. You shouldn't take normal suggestions on how to do your job better as being picked on."

The boss showed her letters from the angry clients and described the messes that had resulted when she and the other girls made mistakes. "What the problem is, Janet," the boss concluded, "isn't our trying to make your life difficult. It is our trying to run this place professionally and efficiently with as few mistakes as possible. To do that, we need your cooperation and understanding."

It took Janet some time to understand that she had been thin-skinned. When she did, she made fewer mistakes and the feeling of being "picked on" faded away.

Our lack of imagination in failing to see how good, constructive advice from our boss can help us move forward can hamper us. It makes all the difference in the world when we see it as constructive advice and not as personal, unmerited carping.

Make reporting to your boss a success step

Did you ever take a special course on "How to Report to Your Boss"? The chances are you've developed your type of reporting to your boss purely from experience. Are you doing it correctly? Are you making it another success step on your way up in the business world?

Here are some pointers to keep in mind:

1. Accept reporting to your boss as a normal, routine function of your job.

2. See it as a continuous opportunity to keep your boss aware of the good work you are doing.

3. Use it as an opportunity to get the boss's advice on how to correct situations in which you are having trouble.

4. Don't be casual about your reporting; take it seriously, but do it easily and in a relaxed manner.

5. Use the method of stating again what the assignment was, your method of going about it, the amount of time involved, and what the present results have been. The boss will be interested in knowing what the costs involved are if money is part of the assignment.

6. Fill the boss in on anything new that has developed.

7. Don't gloss over any unhappy facts; tell the boss the truth.

8. Have a note pad ready, and when you've finished your brief report, be ready to write down the boss's suggestions and comments. Writing things down shows your boss you want to be organized to tackle all of the remaining details and to get instructions for new assignments.

9. When you're finished, leave. Don't drag the reporting session out. You can always tell when the session is over in the boss's mind. You and the boss both have things to do. Get out and get busy.

Effective reporting to your boss essentially is keeping the boss well informed of what is going on in your area. The more informed you keep your boss, the more respect you earn. Gaining greater respect from your boss through this single method is another success step upward for you.

Why your boss can't always
pay attention to you

Some days your boss doesn't seem to be aware that you're around the place. You wonder, "Have I done something wrong?" Or, "Yesterday, the boss said hello to me. Today I'm ignored. What's going on?"

When your boss doesn't seem to notice you on certain days, don't get in a dither. Be understanding. Your boss has peak periods where there is much to take into consideration. There are many things on your boss's mind.

There can be serious problems to deal with, unexpected meetings to get ready for, unexpected visitors coming in an hour, small and large crises to cope with, perhaps personal problems at home. All these and more can take the boss's mind away from you for hours and days.

If you are "left out" during these periods, don't fret. It is actually a sort of compliment to you. The boss regards you as "safe" and running under your own momentum. The boss doesn't feel that you require attention. The boss feels that you can be turned away from for a while without fear that you'll fall on your face or cause a problem.

Your imagination can get you into trouble when your boss fails to pay attention to you. You'll conjure up all sorts of wrong ideas of what's going on. Fight the impulse. Stick by the old business rule that what counts isn't what you imagine the boss is thinking but what the boss *does*.

Order will quickly be restored when your boss gets things ironed out and comes back to the "Good morning, how are you?" attentiveness.

Catching your boss's eye
by being highly visible

Ethel wasn't exactly shy, but she didn't like to call attention to herself. She had a habit of virtually slinking to her desk every morning. She preferred anonymity. It never occurred to her to stick her head in her boss's office and say, "Good morning!"

An excellent worker, she had hopes of getting a promotion that was pending. She needed the extra money and, after all, she'd worked for the company for over ten years. She felt she deserved it.

The promotion went to Charlotte. Ethel nearly went up in smoke. When she calmed down, her good sense made her study Charlotte's office manners. For the first time, Ethel saw Charlotte as an individual and not just someone who also worked in the group. She made notes. Charlotte did these things:

1. Said hello to everyone in the group, the boss included.
2. Had her coffee break with several other people, rather than alone at her desk as Ethel did.
3. Routinely went in to see the boss to report and ask for advice.
4. Dressed well and looked exceptionally attractive although she wasn't nearly as pretty as Ethel.
5. Brought birthday cards and inexpensive gifts to others in the group who celebrated birthdays.
6. Smiled often, laughed easily, and listened attentively to the others instead of sitting in isolation and avoiding the others.
7. Got her assignments done on time and asked the boss for more.

To her credit, Ethel examined herself. It took a great deal of effort on her part, but she began to follow Charlotte's example. In a few months she had made enough progress to be asked to lunch by some of the other people in the group. The boss even stopped at her desk to compliment her on her good work. She responded by saying, "Good morning!" each day to the boss before she sat at her desk.

There wasn't another promotion in sight, but Ethel began to feel like a different person. She liked the idea of being accepted, of being a more lively part of the group. She found, too, that the coffee tasted much better when she joined the others for the morning break.

Being highly visible to your boss doesn't mean cheap theatrics. It means being your natural self. It means coming out of your shell to meet the rest of the world. In the long run, being highly visible in a normal way means making progress in the business world.

It means setting yourself up to get more enjoyment and satisfaction out of your job.

Try taking on some of your boss's responsibilities

Your boss is being paid to do a job. Why should you take on some of your boss's responsibilities? Why should you edge into the boss's territory?

The point isn't that you do the boss's work. *The point is that you try to find ways to help the boss.* Ways such as these:

1. Methods for increasing the group's overall productivity.
2. Ways to prevent costly mistakes from being made.
3. Ways to cut down waste of supplies and time and expenditure of money.
4. Ways to do old practices better, more efficiently.
5. Entirely new ways, perhaps revolutionary, of getting work done.
6. Acquisition of new equipment to help speed things up and establish greater accuracy.

Finding ways to help the boss isn't difficult. You just have to keep the "help" thought in your mind. The "help" thought goes like this: "My boss is very busy. My boss can't think of everything. My boss can use all good ideas and suggestions for improving the performance of our group. I'm out here on the firing line. I'll keep an eye open for better ways to do things. I'll take any good ideas I get to the boss."

You're not encroaching on your boss's territory. You're

helping your boss get a firmer grip. Your good boss will appreciate your interest in taking on some of the responsibilities. *It is an appreciation that will pay dividends to you.*

Spread your enthusiasm and give your boss a boost

Marianne worked for the director of research for a nationwide trade association in a local group of twelve people. She heard all the standard complaints. The association was a dead end, members were dropping out and not paying their substantial dues, government regulations would run them out of business, the executives were all self-serving idiots, and so on.

She refused to become pessimistic. She observed just the opposite. The association was actually becoming stronger and more representative of its members, new members *were* coming in, the government regulations weren't all that restrictive, and the executives were hard-working and conscientious.

She felt enthusiastic about what the association was trying to do and she was understanding of the difficulties it faced. She went to her boss. She pointed out that while the association had an excellent newsletter for its members, covering its activities, legislation, and industry news, there was no national newsletter for the employees in the various offices across the country. She offered to be a contributor for her group if the boss could convince the brass that one was needed for everyone in the association's offices.

In two months, a newsletter was born. The executive director wrote her a note. The key sentence: "I don't know why we didn't think of this before, since it's so obvious that we have long needed one. We thank you for bringing its necessity to our attention."

Marianne's enthusiasm paid off. It spread to the others in the group and through the entire staff of the association. The result was a more cohesive work group and a boost for her boss.

Her next pay raise showed clearly it was also a boost for Marianne.

What do you do when your boss is in emotional trouble?

For many years we've been aware of the emotional problems that women have during the menopause period. A woman boss in this time of her life can be difficult to cope with. Lately, quite a bit of attention has been given to men between the ages of thirty-five and fifty-five who become emotionally unstable during what is variously called the male climacteric, the male menopause, the middle-age slump, and the middle-age syndrome.

The female menopause arrives when a woman's reproductive capacity comes to an end and her ovaries fail to produce a normal amount of hormonal secretion. An estrogen deficiency upsets her nervous system and she can become nervous or depressed or suffer headaches, choking sensations, and other physical and mental disorders. Fortunately, there are medical and surgical corrections available.

The man's problem is that his hormone supply, testosterone, has declined, resulting in a deep psychological fall. Basically, the man has quite suddenly seen the end of the road somewhere up ahead. He has slowed down, realized that he is mortal—that what he believed was eternal youth is gone, that he is in a race with time. He has new circumstances to cope with, his energies are fading, and his fantasies about his "great successes" are in need of overhauling.

This male boss can quickly become depressed, convinced that life has lost its meaning, that he somehow has ended up with the short stick. He may begin to drink heavily, chase the girls, or cause trouble at home by incessant arguing with his wife. He often is excessively worried about losing his sex drive.

Male or female bosses in the throes of these terrible emotional problems are extremely difficult to work with. They don't mean to be difficult, naturally, but they often are gripped with nearly uncontrollable emotional forces. Equally important, some of them may be immensely disappointed that they are in the "out group" as far as top management is concerned and not with the "in group" of politicians in the office or plant. These people can become terribly sour on life and on the business world in equal amounts.

How do you cope with a boss who is in this sort of emotional trouble? First is awareness. Does your boss become easily depressed, flighty, irritable without proper cause? What spoken clues does your boss give you? The boss's behavior will alert you by what is said and done.

Second, use compassion. The course of life is such that all of us reach these middle-age difficulties. Because your boss has them doesn't mean your boss is unusual or abnormal or that he is cracking up. It means you are required to be patient, considerate, and very tactful. Often a boss does not *realize* what is happening.

Third, don't add to the difficulties. Be diplomatic, but stick firmly to your guns when you know what work must be done. Your job is to help your boss get the work done. The difficulties will eventually be overcome and your considerate help will be appreciated by the boss.

Coping with a boss who is entangled in middle-age change of life is not easy by any means. It is all on a highly charged emotional level, and your instinct is to avoid involvement. Whatever the problem in your case, don't run away. Do the best you can, even if it means a very confidential talk with your boss's boss about the situation, a sincere talk aimed at helping your boss untangle the sticky net of the middle-age syndrome.

How can you tell a truly responsive boss from a fake?

Sincerity can be faked, but not forever. There are phoneys in the business world who try to convince you that they have your best interests in mind. What these characters want is *to use you* to further their self-interest. How can you tell the really good boss from the phoney? Here are some examples of how these business con artists operate:

1. This fake headed a small company making metal parts. He exhorted everyone with the slogan, "We're going to grow!" He promised a lot, but the payoff was always "When we get bigger." The company did grow, and this fake suddenly sold out to a larger company, taking a nice big job with them and leaving his workers to face the inevitable "pruning" and rearrangements by the new management team from another city. *Fakes are great at promises.*

2. This division vice president of a plastics company kept a very talented sales manager from leaving for a better job by saying, "I'm training you to be my successor. You'll get my job when I move up." Because the sales manager was good, the vice president was able to record an impressive profit record. But when he moved up, he recommended that the trusting sales manager be *replaced! Fakes are great at treachery.*

3. This charlatan persuaded the research and development group this boss headed in a large consumer product company to work evenings and weekends "to meet the do-it-or-else objectives top management has laid on me. Help get this job done, and we'll all go places." With syrupy pleadings, he conned the group into extensive efforts that produced some fine products. He didn't tell them, naturally, that he was taking all of the credit for their efforts and that in fact there had been no do-it-or-else edict from top management. He had been trying to make *himself* look good. He won a promotion, leaving his stunned group wondering why they had been so taken in. *Fakes are great at self-promotion at the expense of others.*

4. This lady ran a public relations agency. In her haste to make money for herself, she deliberately underpaid her account executives, most of whom were women. She told them that she had to build a cash reserve while she built the agency. When their cumulative efforts achieved this result, did she

raise salaries and improve working conditions? She merged the agency with a bigger one, and the accounts were taken over by the newcomers. Half of her account executives were out looking for jobs in a short time. *Fakes can be heartless.*

Trust between you and your boss is one of the most precious ingredients of your work day. Trust is built by the sincerity which you both display. A truly responsive boss would never take advantage of your mutual trust. Fakes will promise and not deliver. Fakes will be treacherous, greedy, and heartless because they *will* take advantage of those who trust them. It's part of their life style.

Many a trusting person has believed what the fake boss said. When they were let down and asked the boss about those attractive promises, they were told, "Well, things have changed," or, "It just didn't work out," or, "You misunderstood what I said." It is an unfortunate part of the business world that many people *are* led down the garden path. Sometimes the boss does mean to fulfill a promise but sees an opportunity to further his or her self-interest. There goes the promise, poof!

You can tell a truly responsive boss from a fake by paying attention to what the boss does and not what the boss says. If the boss *does* what the boss says, and in a reasonable time, that boss is truly responsive. If the boss keeps stringing things out for a long time, with little or no action to carry out promises, *that boss is suspect.*

If your instincts tell you that you are being conned, don't wait. Sit down with your boss and try to get those fine promises in writing. Get the situation cleared up. It is one thing to be trusting, another to be duped. If the boss won't put it in writing, you've been served an early notice that *that* boss does not intend to carry out the promises.

Trust your instincts. You'll know when a boss is truly responsive to your needs. You'll *sense* when you're being conned. The decision is tough: stay or get out, but the decision is yours. Your instincts will tell you which way to go.

Help your boss and
you help yourself

Even when they have a truly responsive boss, a lot of people in the business world can't seem to get it through their heads that when they help their boss they end up helping themselves. The reason is that they have a narrow, selfish view of the business world—the "what's in it for me?" view.

What's in it for *you* when you help your responsive boss is that you make yourself more visible to your boss, you show yourself in a better light, you prove that you are worth the boss's interest, you show that you merit pay raises and promotions. *That's what's in it for you.*

Think of our theme: Establish friendly, harmonious, productive relations with your boss and open new opportunities for yourself. Opportunities are worthless unless you take advantage of them. Take advantage of the opportunities afforded by your responsive, friendly boss. Become involved in the boss's goals. Find ways to help the boss achieve those goals. *You'll find you're not giving, you're getting.*

You'll find, too, that as you work to find ways to help your boss, you're acquiring more experience, more insight, more skills, more knowledge, more stability, more security, more optimism, more enthusiasm.

In other words, you're busy helping yourself move forward in the business world.

8

Put Your Entire Group to Work for You

You've come to the easy-to-reach conclusion that there will always be other people around you at work. Unless you're occupying a solitary forest-ranger tower in the mountains, you're surrounded by others in your group. How can you put this collection of widely different people to work for you? Start with two fundamentals:

1. You are exposed to the subtle influences of those around you and the pressure of the group. You are susceptible to both the impact of the individuals and the impact of them all weighed together. This is called "peer pressure," and it is very much a force with which you must deal.

2. You both love and hate the individuals because of your closeness to them. You're dependent on them because they are there and you must live among them. You're vulnerable to them because they can withdraw their support of you at any moment.

Include your boss. You are more dependent on and vulnerable to your boss than any of the others. Let's see what you can do to protect yourself against these dependency and vulnerability factors. Let's see how you can put most of the people, if not all, to work for you.

Assess the others in your group

Have you taken the others for granted? Are they just people to you? Do you lump them all together, like a candy bridge mix of humans? It's one of the worst mistakes you can make. Here's how you go about assessing the others in your group:

1. You understand that none of them are at all different emotionally from you.

2. Each of them is afraid of something—failure, exposure, responsibility, change, even success.

3. Each wants recognition as an individual—some evidence that you appreciate them, understand them, are aware of them.

4. Their self-interest is far more important to them than their interest in you.

5. They have needs of an astonishing variety, with the basic ones paralleling your own needs.

6. It is in your best self-interest to learn their characteristics and to treat them each in a specific individual manner—in short, to cope with them not as a lump of people but as separate human beings.

It is a temptation to sort your coworkers into two groups. One group you judge to be favorable to you. The other group includes those who you feel might not be favorable to you. This is another mistake. You can't ever tell precisely who is for you or against you in the business world. You can judge only by what they say and do. You can't read their minds and know exactly how they feel about you.

The best action on your part is to accept them as individuals and go one-on-one to make friends with them. You can nullify potential problem people by making a consistent effort to be friendly to them. You can earn more recognition from those who instinctively like you by doing the same thing with them.

Your assessment starts with an effort to avoid disliking anyone in your group because they're men, women, young, old, white, black, brown, of different religion, of different ideology, or for any such standard discriminatory reason. Following that, you make every effort to establish a good working relationship with them. The key thought of this is the understanding that they are *another you*. They just don't look and act like you.

There's no way you can win all by yourself

I've met some vigorous people who felt they didn't need anyone else in order to succeed in the business world. They regarded others with a light contempt, a haughty intolerance. They felt that the others were small hurdles to be stepped over—ignored more than noticed.

It can't be done that way. You know that. You realize that you can get further in the business world by "using" other people. Here are some of the ways you "use" the others in your group to benefit yourself:

▪ Each of these persons is a specialist in some line of work, and you can learn their specialties from them; you're a student, they're the teachers.

▪ They challenge you to do better because you'll learn to respect their specialties; the more you learn from them, the more skilled you become.

▪ You'll profit from their objective criticism when you come to see it as not being nit-picking or grousing.

▪ They'll give you feedback which helps you determine the results of your efforts.

▪ You learn more about established rules and practices from

them than from the boss; they're on the firing line and know the score.

You need everyone in your group. Despite the human problems of people working together, you can turn each of them into a plus for yourself. You use the Golden Rule, *you treat each of them the way you want them to treat you.* It's that simple.

How your group can block your progress

Many a hard-headed person running to catch the success train has been tripped up and thrown by the members of the group. How can your group block your progress? Easily, by any of these (and other) devices:

- The rumor mill, which spreads complaints that you are hard to get along with, that there's something phoney about you.
- Letting you dangle when an emergency turns up and you need their immediate help; their deliberate procrastination can murder you.
- Not giving you the proper advice at a critical time when you need it.
- Blocking you in your assignments by making it appear to your boss that you're the one who is holding up everyone else.
- Setting up situations where you come under stress and tension.

There is no end to what the others in your group can do to block you if they collectively get down on you. There is a lesson in capital letters for you in that sentence. Pay attention to it.

You can win your group's enthusiastic support

It can be done, but it takes a whale of a lot of work on your part. The support of those in your group is never freely given to you. You must earn it. How do you do this? Your game plan includes these plays:

1. *Constantly think of yourself as a leader, not a follower* This is your ego reinforcement that will be reflected in the way you conduct yourself with others. You can't be meek and subservient and win people's respect. You can't be overbearing, either; a real leader is never abrasive or domineering.

2. *Pay attention to their needs* As we've said, they fear some things and deeply desire others. Seek the answers to what troubles them and what they want out of their jobs.

3. *Don't let them down* If they confide in you, keep it to yourself. If they ask for reasonable favors, give them and be quiet about it. If you promise them anything, follow through and deliver.

4. *Stay unflappable* Your calmness in crisis periods is like a port in a storm. When they goof, be sympathetic and help them correct the situation. Coolness under fire is a greatly admired trait.

5. *Make decisions* One of the worst labels they can pin on you is that you can't make up your mind. When you avoid making decisions because you fear failure, you lose respect. You can't afford that.

6. *Listen to them* If you do all the talking, you're a loser. A winner knows when to talk and when to shut up and listen. Besides, you learn more listening than you do talking. You're a learner, remember.

7. *Communicate* Fill them in on the essential details. Let them know what your assignments are, how you're doing, where you need help. Ask them for advice and get their feedback. You've heard of two-way communications. Keep everything to yourself, and you cut off this flow of feedback information. Why block yourself?

8. *Keep your identity* Don't try to blend into the landscape. Be yourself, stay with your life style. If you imitate others, you become a meaningless carbon copy.

9. *Fine-tune your sense of responsibility* Show them that when you take on assignments, you're going to deliver. Procrastination isn't in your dictionary. You're a producer, interested in achieving objectives.

10. *Be friendly* There's a difference between acting friendly and being friendly. Your group knows this. Honest friendliness on your part goes a long way toward winning your group's support.

Certainly you'll be disappointed that some of your plays will be stopped cold. Some people may never come around to supporting you. That's part of the game; win some, lose some. You keep trying, knowing that's what makes champions.

You can make friends out of "distant" people

Usually, when you find people are distant to you, you turn away from them. You have other things to do. Why bother trying to make friends out of clods, stonewalls, frozen faces, and emotional ice cubes?

You can make friends out of these people who *seem* to want to put distance between you and them. *You realize that no one absolutely wants to be cut off from other people.* Those who appear to be emotional ice cubes have just never been able to unlock their warmth and affection. They're just as emotional inside as you are. They have difficulty expressing their emotions.

Distant people are simply trying to protect themselves from you and the others. They fear involvement because they feel that they'll be "exposed" and found to be unworthy of your interest. They fear you'll let them down—pull the rug out from under them—if they get too close to you in a friendly sense.

You make friends of these emotionally handicapped people in the same way that you do with anyone else. You smile at them, even if they don't return the smile. You say, "Good morning!" to them even if they don't respond. You show interest in what they do in the group. You compliment them at appropriate times. You try to find out what interests them in their free time.

The going will be slow, but the results will be the same. You'll find that there is a friend behind every gloomy face. Don't wait for them; take them on and win them over. The rule: *No one you meet, no matter how distant the person appears to be, is ever unworthy of your interest and attention.*

Understanding the person who won't fit into the group

Sometimes they're called "rugged individualists," "loners," or "operators." They are persons with different goals and different values from those of most of the people in your group. They just don't seem to fit into the group.

These persons don't respond to peer pressure the way the rest do. They seem to be obsessed with an urgency that escapes the others. Some of them are everywhere, poking their noses into other people's territories. Some of them do their work in an entirely different way from the others and achieve better results.

Some of them appear to be cold, unfriendly, and uninterested in people, but excited about the challenge of beating schedules, setting up new procedures, opening new adventures, or topping achievements others have scored. They don't mix well, seldom join the group in the trivial things that make work livable, and obviously have set themselves apart deliberately.

You accept them for what they are, people who don't fit into the group. There's nothing wrong with that. They fit *somewhere* in the business world. Despite their standoffishness, be friendly and helpful to them. They're marching to a different drumbeat, and they sometimes end up being the real innovators and doers.

Show your group that you appreciate them

Why is it up to *you* to show appreciation of the others in your group? Because *you're the one who wants to go someplace in the business world.* You're like a politician running for office. The game of success can't be played any other way.

Remember the others on their birthdays with greeting cards, a rose on their desk, or whatever. Spend time with them at coffee breaks, lunch time, when you meet in the hallway.

Help them develop their abilities, help them solve their problems, help them with their self-improvement needs. You're an alert person, and you can spot opportunities to step in and help without it being out of place or offensive. Your friendliness and genuine interest will show them that you appreciate them as individuals.

What's your payoff? You can easily answer that question yourself.

What you learn when you study your group's resources

We're often so concerned about ourselves that we don't notice the rich resources of the people within our group. Added up, the total work capabilities of any group can be impressive. It is this total sum that is of interest to you in your activities to get ahead in the business world. Here are some points:

1. You learn that people will help you when they feel you are deserving of their help.

2. Each of them has a specialty or two, and it is of value to you to have them teach you something of those specialties.

3. Most people want to see others succeed, but not at their own expense.

4. People aren't constant masses; they are caught in slow, subtle changes that can be spotted only over years, not days.

5. People have many emotional hangups that stymie their own progress; these are evident in their absenteeism, hypochondria, and psychosomatic illnesses.

6. Unless you make friends of them, some jealous people will become backstabbers in their efforts to take you down a peg or two.

7. Everyone, to some degree, resents changes in work patterns or situations. Change is never warmheartedly welcomed.

The resources are there, but they are covered in many areas with layers of human inertia, stubbornness, resistance, and resentment. It is your job to peel these layers away and put the resources to work for you. You're the one who is going places, and this layer-peeling is part of the challenge that success poses for you.

Put your boss
to work for you

Your boss obviously is part of your group—the most important part. One of your major goals is to establish your boss's trust in you. In relation to your group, here is how you can put your boss to work for you:

1. By showing your boss how well you're "making it" with the group

2. By the greater productivity you'll have because the people in the group are working with you and not against you

3. By putting a spotlight on your leadership qualities within the group, qualities that earn you attention for the next promotion or pay raise

4. By your effectiveness in improving the climate for progress within the group

In other words, your efforts to win the group over to you will be noticed by the boss. You see this as a triangle: you, the boss, and the group. The triangle is a sort of electrical circuit. It works only when the circuit is properly connected. You're the generator, the group acts as the wires (or conductors), and the boss is the light bulb that responds to the electric energy.

Showing your group that you know what you're doing

Without saying a word, you can show your group that you know what you're doing. In these ways:
- Taking the initiative for getting work done
- Being concise in what you say so that your message is understood
- Being persuasive about your good ideas
- Making decisions
- Managing your time effectively
- Acting calmly under pressure
- Being mature
- Working every day to cut costs
- Asking questions when you need information
- Maintaining positive attitudes
- Being disciplined and organized
- Listening when others are trying to say something
- Working at increasing your productivity
- Taking on anything that will increase your knowledge and skills

Understanding the variations of people in your group

We tend to like people who "are like me." In the business world you seldom have the opportunity to select those persons in your group. You take them as you find them. It is up to you to understand them and the wide variations they represent. The basic ones are these:

1. Widows and widowers Not everyone has the good fortune to have his or her marriage untouched by death before the normal time. Widows and widowers carry on the best they can, many of them suffering from deep loneliness.

2. *The beginners* If they are college graduates, they often have to be retrained to meet the realities of the business world. They need help in coping with the strange structures and practices they find on the job.

3. *The single men* There are more unmarried men in business now than ever before. Some just haven't found the "right woman." Others don't plan on getting married for a long while. Others have boyfriends instead of girlfriends. Some are "Momma's boys" who are afraid of involvement with women because they don't trust their masculinity.

4. *Married men* They have families to raise, homes to buy, and college tuitions and taxes to pay. Some like to play around, but by far the biggest percentage are hard-working, dedicated men who conduct the marriage game properly and are exceedingly fine persons.

5. *Married women* They'd almost all rather be home, but with the new liberation atmosphere, they find they can enjoy more material things and more security if they work. They have resented not being paid the same salary for doing the same work that men do. This discrimination aspect has been resolved by federal legislation. The 35 million women in the business world today are a massive force and they do outstanding work. They are not only employees, but wives, mothers, taxpayers, commuters, housemaids, and all that. Their days are busy from morning to late night. Many of them are discovering their own identities.

6. *The near-retirements* Sunset people, senior citizens, whatever they are called, these men and women are near the end of their full-time working days. Retirement means they will soon leave your group. Some will get part-time jobs, others (more fortunate) will enjoy the pension or profit-sharing benefits. No one ever really wants to retire, and many of them are depressed, disenchanted, fearful of what lies ahead. Most of them failed to see their idealized dreams of success turn out the way they had dreamed. They've been around a long time, and they can provide you with a wealth of helpful background information.

7. *The unmarried woman* We talked about Ms. in a previous chapter. The main point here is that the unmarried woman today has more opportunities for advancement in the business world than ever before, at better pay. The fact that so many of them have an excellent education and that they are ready to challenge the business system bodes for some interesting years ahead.

How does your group relate to the entire organization?

Is your group a real spark-plug outfit? Does it hold the attention of the rest of the organization? Does it get recognition, or is it an obscure department, half-ignored?

What have been the past experiences of the group? Has it been changed frequently by top management in an effort to make it function properly? Has it had a succession of bosses in the last five or ten years?

If your group is playing a key role in the operation of the entire organization, fine. If not, you might look for a better place to hop to. Sinking ships are no fun.

But if you feel your boss knows the score and is making progress, that the group has settled down and is working together, then you may want to gamble that it will become a winner.

It is worth your time to analyze the group and its overall chances of making it big within the organization.

Coping with people who protect their territory

Nearly everyone has an instinct to protect their little bit of turf at work. Some take this protectiveness very seriously, others are more mild about it. You have to cope with this human element in your efforts to hold down big and small hostilities and make progress for yourself in the business world.

Agnes was an excellent secretary, and her male boss traveled quite often. She developed the habit of using his office to make personal phone calls where others wouldn't eavesdrop on her conversations. One day the boss returned sooner than expected and found her sitting at his desk, smoking and using the phone.

The boss clouded up and stormed at what he felt was an unwarranted use of his office (his turf). From that day their working relationship deteriorated, and it wasn't long before the boss arranged for Agnes' transfer elsewhere. He should have been more tolerant, but he was territory-minded.

Most people resent any intrusion of their job authority. They guard their rights and responsibilities with determination to keep others out and thus protect their job security. Hostilities arise in *this* area more than in any other.

You've already developed a sense of awareness of how people feel about their little piece of the business world. You want to protect your own turf, don't you? Just don't become overly protective to the point where you develop hostility toward anyone you feel is encroaching. Turf isn't all that important. It's what people *do* on the turf that means something.

How do you handle the emotional firecrackers?

There are some people who seem to have their fuse lighted nearly all the time. These are *emotional firecrackers,* and you may have one or more of them in your group. How do you handle them without getting a temperamental explosion?

Here's the way your thinking should go:

1. *You* are never selected as a single target for their tantrums. Such people want the *entire world* to sympathize with them. You just happen to be handy.

2. They allow their tempers to explode, mostly in muted pops, because they want *attention*.

3. They are, in effect, saying, "No one pays any attention to me, so *I'll make them!*"

4. They want attention because they feel the world has been *unjust* to them. They feel they've been cheated. They enjoy playing the role of a person who's been victimized.

5. Some of them have developed the unconscious habit of doing things or setting up situations which cause others to criticize or chastise them. Then they can say, "See? What did I tell you! Everyone picks on me!"

The best course you can take is to ignore their temper pops. Their tiny firecrackers of emotional outbursts are relatively harmless. Concentrate on their good features. Be understanding of them. Never retaliate. Don't take them seriously unless they really get out of hand. Then say, "I know how tough it's been for you, and I sympathize. But let's get on with the work at hand, okay?" That should poop the pops for the moment.

Who said you had to love your company?

We're all a little nutty when it comes to something with which we identify. Our neighborhood has to be the best. Our car must be an attractive eye-catcher. Our home has to be better than those of our friends. The company we work for, just because we work there, has to be among the best.

When we choose something, we want to believe that we chose the finest from the selection available to us. It's an individual I'm-better-than-anyone-else emotion which is hard to resist.

No one has ever said that because you chose to work for your present company you absolutely had to love the company. A lot of heartache could be avoided if we would learn a simple truth about American business. As different as they all seem to be, most companies are almost all nearly alike.

Any company will let you down if you expect too much from it. Your company has been changing from the day you started to the present day. What you took for granted as a "right" with a company can be taken away from you.

What you regarded as the best company to work for can easily end up being the worst company. Not because the company changed that much, but because *you* changed. You came to work that first day with illusions and misunderstandings. Since you found out that things were different from what you expected (it takes some people years to find out!), you're unhappy. You think the company let you down.

All companies will let you down if you set yourself up for a letdown. What they're buying and what you're selling is experience. You can honestly love your company if you're treated fairly, if you're let in on some of the decision-making that affects your job, if you're given sufficient pay, security, and opportunities for advancement. If not, you don't have to love your company.

Many very successful people have detested their companies, but they fought for their self-interests and won in spite of the situation. You can do the same thing with any company where you work, love it or not.

You can motivate those whom you supervise

How do you motivate a mule? You'll never have to do this, but the question is a good one because it shows that mules, like people, motivate themselves.

An extremely successful businessman once said, "Never forget the self-interest of the employee." It's all there in his statement. You motivate those whom you supervise by working to help them achieve what *they* want in the business world. Every employee has certain needs, and these must be satisfied or there is no motivation for that person to help you achieve *your* goals.

What do we call "self-interest"? The most important elements in a person's self-interest are these:

1. *Acceptance* by the group at the office or the plant
2. *Approval* for the work that is done properly
3. *Control* over some of the processes that affect workloads and methods of getting the work done
4. *Worthiness,* which comes from a sense of satisfaction that the work is leading to that person's goals
5. *Security,* which is money or possessions that protect that person from going without or suffering hardships
6. *Achievement* of meaningful objectives
7. *Self-appreciation,* which is the feeling that they're "making it"

How do you know what someone wants from you to better his or her self-interest? Listen and observe. As we've said before, they'll tell you or show you by their actions. It's your job to find ways to help those whom you supervise to find satisfaction for these personal needs on the job.

How to handle very young people in your group

Every year high school and college graduates join us in the business world. We like to call them "the kids." They have no pressure groups fronting for them. They're "overqualified" if they have impressive college degrees, "wet behind the ears" if they're fresh from high school; they "get in our way" because the business world is strange to them.

How quickly *we* forget the days when we left high school or college to enter the mysterious and frightening world of industry or commerce. We forget because we want to forget. Yet, all of us remember how there were *some* helping hands extended to us to pull us over some of the rocky ground, to get us started in the right direction.

The former students who join us today aren't "kids." They're young men and women. They're better educated, and they can contribute handsomely to the business world.

You can handle these young people in your group by following a very simple guideline. Just remember how much *you* appreciated help from the more established people when you went to work. Then get busy and find unpatronizing ways to give the newcomers that help.

Your friendly attitude helps them, you feel good about it, and your group is strengthened. *Your boss will notice,* and you'll win more brownie points.

You might become an adopted parent

That's right. Some people in your group may become attached to *you* in their unconscious search for a substitute figure representing a father, a mother, an older brother or sister, an uncle or an aunt, or a fantasy person. How's that again?

Look at it this way. Not all in your group are that much in control of their emotions. The business world is as tough for them to accept and live in as it is for you. Your collective boss may be too remote and cool for them to adopt as an authority figure. They may be afraid of the boss, for a wide variety of reasons. So they look for *someone they see every day* who can be a substitute mother or father or other symbolic figure.

They don't come right out and say, "Hey, I've adopted you because you remind me of my father (or mother)." They don't *realize* that this is what they've done. It's just that somewhere in the mysterious way the mind works they find they cotton to you and look up to you as they would the authority figure you seem to represent.

Most often these people will be younger than you. They may bring their problems to you, seeking your advice. They may seem to be under foot an unnecessary amount of time.

If you sense that you have become an adopted authority figure, take it as a compliment. After all, we're on this earth to help others as well as to help ourselves. Pay some attention to them, help them, keep it under control, and you'll end up with more friends. What's wrong with that?

Smoothing out your blooper that affects your group

You make a mistake, and it causes a problem for your group. Your first reaction is to be enormously unhappy with yourself. Your second reaction is to see how the rest of the people in your group are taking it. Your third reaction is to come up with an excuse for what happened.

These reactions are humanly normal. We all follow the pattern. There is, however, an effective way to smooth out any blunder you make which affects your group.

First, say to yourself, "I haven't made many such mistakes. I made this one and no one else. I take complete responsibility for it."

Second, say to the others, "Well, I won't make *that* mistake again!" Say it in good humor, with a smile (if you can!).

Third, get to work setting things right. Ask for help if you need it. Your immediate objective is to correct the situation, not make it worse.

You've heard the expressions, "Man is a mistake-maker," "We learn from the mistakes we make," "No one goes through life without making mistakes," and "Everything I learned to do right I learned by first doing it wrong." No one is exempt from making mistakes, so there is no reason for you to thrash yourself mentally.

Take your blooper in stride and get on with life.

How to enjoy misery
of your own making

You've heard that old saying, "He's enjoying poor health?" Glen worked out a system on the job that enabled him to enjoy misery, all of his own making.

Here are the guidelines he used to make it work:

1. He expected everyone to do what he wanted them to do.

2. He regarded everyone as a mechanical device that was devoid of emotions and feeling.

3. He acted as if he was the only one in the group who had any idea worth consideration.

4. He felt it was a waste of time to listen to anyone else.

5. He felt women had no place in the business world.

6. He regarded his boss as a nincompoop, and undercut the boss at every turn.

7. He showed up very early at the office, stayed until everyone left, and lost no opportunity to remind everyone that he was at the office on Saturdays while they took the day off.

8. He was a whirling dervish, mixing himself into everyone's work, giving freely of his unsolicited advice and criticism.

9. He missed few chances to boast about his work and what it meant to the organization. He made it clear that nothing would run if he weren't on hand.

Glen could never understand why he was passed over for promotions, why his pay raises came so infrequently, why no one in the group seemed to care about him or his great business expertise.

Glen, in the purest sense, enjoyed a beautiful abrasive misery of his own making. But you've already learned to avoid such misery, haven't you?

Should you confide in your boss and the others?

You spend a third of your day working for a living. You're with your group and your boss during the fattest part of the day. It's natural for you to assume a close relationship with a selected few of them, even with your good boss. Should you confide in them when it comes to your personal life?

Let's start with your boss. The answer is *no*, if you simply want to enlist the boss's sympathy and get unearned help. The answer is *yes* if you're deeply troubled by a group situation which has caused a personal but on-the-job problem for you. An example of the latter would be if you catch a jealous someone telling barefaced lies about you.

This sort of thing isn't big enough to disrupt the group's work, but it is big enough to disrupt *yours*. You can confide in your boss, explaining how you feel and what you think caused this potentially damaging situation. The boss probably won't do anything, but establishing such awareness in the boss's mind will work to keep the rumor mill from coloring the boss's view of you.

Sheer personal things, like trouble with your spouse, trouble involving your children, or embarrassing situations, you should keep to yourself. It's your job to solve them, not your boss's. Anyway, you're not unique; everyone has *some* personal problems.

Never, *never*, go to your boss and confide that you've heard some gossip *about the boss!* Whatever you hear of this nature, forget it. There's no better way to put yourself in your boss's icebox than to relay "things I've heard about you" to your boss.

Now, about the others in your group. Confiding your personal affairs to them can be dangerous. It is dangerous in a small way because, while you may trust an individual with whom you feel close, not all can be trusted to keep your personal secrets to themselves.

I recall being mildly shocked when a coworker told me some

really wild stories about a guy I'll call Ed. They were bizarre enough to be unbelievable. "Who told you all that?" I said. "Ed did," the storyteller answered. I thought it was a put-on until I had lunch with Ed one day. Without any prompting from me, Ed went into an elaborate description of the same problems. My estimate of Ed went down to zero.

People such as Ed, who freely tell their innermost secrets, are just asking to be mentally kicked by their coworkers. Perhaps they're unconsciously seeking to be rejected. Some people do have a persistent habit of trying to get the world down on them. Don't ask me why.

Be extremely careful whom you select as a confidant. Sometimes you're deeply troubled and you want to *talk* to someone about your personal troubles. I suggest you fight the urge to unload your troubles on anyone at the office or plant. There's just too much chance that your troubles will be eagerly passed along to others who you'd just as well not have know about them.

Confiding in anyone is an act of trust. Can you really trust the person in whom you're confiding?

Never leave the office in an angry mood

Let's repeat it, one of your biggest challenges is to manage your frustration. Few days go by without some irritation, some setbacks, some lack of success. You can pick up the virus of pessimism from other people. The trick is not to let these negative emotions rub off on you.

Whatever the day has been, no matter what troubles pounced on you, never leave the office in an angry mood. You're moving from work into your own time. Why clutter up your own time with irritations that came from the job and not from your personal life?

Get out, go home, and enjoy yourself.

9

Drawing Your Map to Find the Treasure of Success

If you wait for other people to make a success out of you, you'll wait a long time. Your boss does represent a golden opportunity for you, as you have seen. It makes no difference whether your boss is a thoroughly unlikable person, a mediocre glob, or a truly fine person. The opportunity is there for you to seize.

You are intelligent and you know that helping the boss achieve the specific goals the boss has in mind *helps you*. You help yourself whenever you help the company you work for. You help yourself to the greatest extent when you draw your own map to find the treasure chest of success that lies hidden somewhere in the foothills of the business world.

Drawing your map to find the treasure chest of success in the work you've chosen to do isn't all that difficult. It seems so because it involves a lot of thinking and planning on your part.

It involves exerting yourself in a wide variety of areas so that you are equipped to take greater responsibility from time to time.

The more skilled you become, the more you move up toward the executive suite. Developing those skills means learning to control yourself, to point yourself consistently in the right direction, and to overcome the obstacles that both you and the business world place in your path.

Let's dig into some of these obstacles, and let's examine some of the mining tools readily available to you.

How computerized are you to make a winning push?

Computers, desk calculators, and ingenious office machines are everywhere. You probably have your share of them where you work. Take a lesson from them. They will operate only as well as they are programmed. The input must be excellent, or the output will be terrible. In the case of computers, for example, you get out of one only what you put into it, but at an incredibly faster rate.

How computerized are you? Have you been working to program yourself with the input that will emerge as the type of success you want? Will you be able to get the big paycheck you want, the nice home, the prestige, the influence and power that is so reassuring to have, because of your planned input into your career?

Computerizing yourself depends on what you are after, how much you want it, and how hard you will work to get it. The lesson here is that any job pays off only to the extent of what we are willing and able to put into it. If you're not computerizing yourself by putting a lot of thought, energy, and zip into your work, get busy.

You're ready to make a winning push, and you win best when you're programmed mentally to do so. The key is *believ-*

ing in yourself. When you strongly believe in yourself, you reduce the human factor of being a stranger to yourself. Being programmed mentally means you are what you believe yourself to be and *that you can become the success you want to become.*

Coping with business world frustrations

There are plenty of frustrations just getting to work. Traffic if you drive, commuting if you take the bus, subway, elevated, or train. These are enough to unsettle any of us.

The most serious frustrations are those of getting your work done and of satisfying your boss. You have the problem of being "typed" as a person. You might be a "cube," which is an advanced state of being square. You might be a swinger, a prima donna, a show-off, a boaster, or a gossip in the eyes of your boss and coworkers. You might be considered a cog in the machine, afraid to speak up and exert yourself, obedient, compliant, someone who occupies space.

There are eyes everywhere in any plant or office. There are ears in all the walls. There is the rumor mill, and it mills you as it does about everyone else. You are vulnerable to what people see, hear, and believe about you, whether it is true or not.

In plain words, you are very visible. If you want to reduce the frustrations of working with other people of all sizes, shapes, complexions, backgrounds, and emotional makeups, you must avoid being passive. You build trust and respect by your actions, by what you do as well as by what you say.

When you exhibit cheerfulness, optimism, and faith in yourself and your work, you build an image of an industrious person who can cope with the complexities of the boss and the job. You demonstrate that insurmountable problems can be solved in an atmosphere of good humor and diligent effort.

Coping with the frustrations in the business world is part of your job. You're being paid for it. It is one of the strongest lines in your treasure map leading toward success.

What conflicting advice does to us

As a youth: "Everyone's smoking cigarettes, why not you?"
As an adult: "Smoking will kill you."
As a child: "Eat your eggs, drink your milk, eat all your butter, eat lots of meat, they're good for you."
As an adult: "Eat that stuff, and cholesterol will help give you a heart attack."
Conflicting advice is part of human existence. Which political candidate to vote for? Should you rent or buy a home? Is frozen fish better than fresh fish? Should you buy something made of wool or buy a synthetic fabric? Should you buy stocks or put your money into bank accounts or real estate? Should you spend now or see inflation take your savings anyway? Should you amass your savings or let Social Security take care of you? Should you buy a new car now despite the high prices or drive your old one into the ground?

In every area of your life you'll be confused by conflicting advice. It is the same way with your job. Should you quit and look elsewhere? Should you seek a transfer? Should you ask for a pay raise or wait until a better time?

Some bosses are great at giving out conflicting information. One boss might say the future looks bright (and you see the sugar plum of a pay raise) and douse it by adding, "if the competition leaves us alone."

Don't expect the system to change. Use your own best judgment after you get all the advice, and come down to the single point: what is best for you?

When the boss wants the impossible out of you

There are times when even the best of bosses will hit the panic button. You may be the key person during one of these crisis periods and your boss may ask the impossible of you. You must do an assignment in a short time, without enough team power behind you, or enough budget, to emerge successfully on target.

Your boss, in a vast desire to accomplish an immediate objective, may be unreasonable, unlistening, unrelenting. The situation is pushing your boss, who feels you must move heaven and earth to help achieve this important objective.

What do you do? You feel definitely that you face a defeat if you go barging right ahead. You don't want to say, "Boss, I can't do it. There isn't enough time. I don't have enough people, and there isn't enough money to make it work right."

Do you face a defeat?

Despite the atmosphere of near-panic, you do these things:

1. Tell your boss you need a "few minutes to evaluate the problem clearly." Go to your office, close the door, and make your notes. What is the problem? What are your options on solving the problem?

2. Once you have a firm, objective grip on what must be done, go back to your boss. You say, "I've done some quick homework, and here are the things that I can do, the things that I cannot do, and here are several alternatives."

3. You stress to your boss that *clear thinking is a must,* that you realize the great importance of the assignment. Your alternatives may be ideas that did not occur to your boss. By treating the emergency situation as a normal event and not as a crisis, you restore some of the semblance of clear thinking to the situation.

4. You say, "Now, evaluating everything connected with this problem, here is the course I suggest you consider for me to

follow." You have put the ball back in his court. The chances are that by removing the "impossible" demand on you, by taking some of the heat out of the situation, you have put yourself in a position to help your boss by going one of the alternative routes and gaining the objective.

You don't have to start running because your boss yells, "Fire!" You don't have to become panicky because your boss has, although it's a very human reaction to do so. Have an emergency plan of your own worked out to help you react calmly to situations of this kind. Go over it in your mind every so often.

You'll be prepared to help your boss when you are needed most, when there is terrific pressure to get certain things done in a rush. You'll not fail, because you're prepared. I'll say it again, being prepared is half of getting any job done no matter how much of a hot potato it might be.

When your boss is hopping mad

Let's say your boss is really teed off about something you've done—or not done.

Whether you're guilty or not, your first job is to get the boss calmed down. The first thing you do is *listen*. When you're confronted and you see that the boss is, indeed, really cranked up about something, don't do any of the following:
1. Start protesting your innocence.
2. Start pointing the finger at someone else.
3. Cloud up and get mad yourself.
4. Walk away in a fuming dudgeon.
5. Cry, if you're inclined to do so.
6. Exhibit an icy indifference.

Listen to what the boss is trying to say. When anyone is hopping mad, he or she seldom chooses words carefully, try as they might. Anger is a loosening emotion. It loosens words most people never use unless they are extremely angry. It also jars loose the angry person's ability to think clearly and logically.

Listen, and let the boss run on until the end of the tirade is reached. Then, and only then, ask questions. Your job is to use your relatively calm head to find out *exactly* what caused the boss to do the lid-flipping bit. Try to keep yourself emotionless. Don't let irritation or distress show on your face or in your words.

If *you* are the guilty person, agree that he or she has every right to be hopping mad. Explain what happened and why. Then state what you will do to set things straight. *This is extremely important.* Use your coolness to think clearly about what can be done to straighten out the mess. If your boss is that mad, there must be a reason. If you honestly are at fault, admit it and come up with a plan to correct the situation.

In a situation like this, the boss has said, without using these words, "Don't you agree that I have a right to be sore about this?" Your boss wants agreement from you, not evasion. Agree, and present a plan of action for immediate consideration.

Now, in the second situation, where you are *not* the guilty person, listen to your boss. You already have an idea of what happened and who is to blame. Loud, indignant protests of innocence won't help you. The best technique is to remain calm, to speak softly and slowly.

Say something like, "You have every right to be mad. I would be just as mad as you. This is a terrible thing to have happen. However, I had absolutely nothing to do with it. Would you like to hear what I believe can be done about it?"

That will switch the tone of things, or certainly should. You've blunted the boss's anger. You've pointed out you're not the guilty person. You've presented *something to consider.* That's the intelligent way to handle a potentially explosive situation.

Fighting anger with anger never works. Your job is to help your boss, and you help most by remaining calm and objective.

It's never easy, but it is one of the things you must do if you're going to continue to improve your lot in the business world.

Find a way to "talk it out"

Along with exercise, which is a splendid method of turning your energy from bad things to good things that will benefit you, there is another method of easing the boss's hold on you. Talk it out with your wife or husband, girlfriend, boyfriend, or parents. A lot of people, I'm afraid, think that talking out frustrations is a sign of weakness. It is a sign of weakness *not* to talk them out.

Medical men have long pointed out that many patients come to them under the pretense of a body ailment when their real purpose is to "get someone to listen to their troubles."

Persons who do this often seek out doctor after doctor and become known in the medical trade as "hypos" or hypochondriacs. They seek in pills what they can't seem to get from their close relatives and friends: a relaxation of their terrible frustrations, hostilities, and depressions and the deep, black moods they get from working for a living.

Why people feel it is a weakness to own up to these emotions is a mystery to me, but they do. Some people do not have anyone to whom they can talk. They have, by fate or by their personalities, been cut away from other people in whom they could confide.

If you're bugged by what's going on where you work, don't cause further trouble to yourself by bottling it up. Get it out of yourself. Talking it over with someone you respect will help drain off these disabling emotions.

Don't wait too long, or you might end up like the horse thief who was caught by a posse in the Old West. With a rope around his neck, he was asked by the sheriff if he had any last words. He nodded. "This has sure taught me a lesson," he said. Don't wait. Talk it out now.

The meaning to you of the "planting cycles"

Look at this simple chart:

15_____20_____ 40_____60_____80 years

I call these "planting cycles," and I've roughed them off into these four periods of years. The meaning to you of these "planting cycles" is this:

1. *Age from 15 to 20* You're finding yourself and trying to diminish your family's hold on you. You're trying out different life styles to see what fits.

2. *Age from 20 to 40* You've picked a life style, and you're busy swimming in the ocean of life. It's heady stuff. Marriage, jobs, new friends, travel, new places, new responsibilities. It goes very fast, but you're standing on your own two feet and making it work.

3. *Age from 40 to 60* Things begin to close in. You haven't done everything you want to do, haven't reaped all the successes you thought you would. Children are growing, demands for more money are increasing, opportunities at work seem to be receding. You see you're not going to make some of your cherished goals. You settle down to make the most of what you have, but you're filled with doubts, anxieties, hostilities, and bitternesses.

4. *Age from 60 to 80* Your love affair with the business world has cooled, but you've found something else, *life*. Your perspective has shifted, and your family, friends, and "fun things" are more important. You travel, dig into new things, become active in areas for which you had no time before in the other cycles. You see where you *did* win an enormous amount from life despite all those setbacks and disappointments.

Each "planting cycle" puts down the seeds for the next cycle. Think of this. It has a very important meaning to you now.

Put this great power to work for you

Optimism is a power you can use. My guess is that you haven't used it as much as you've used the negative power of pessimism. Being pessimistic about things in general, and about work specifically, is an American affliction. It's like a virus that we get just from talking to each other. Add together a bunch of negative comments during a day from yourself and your co-workers, and you go home feeling that work is all a waste of time.

Feeling low about what is happening to you, or around you, is easy. There are so many things that can make you feel low. Too much work, too little time, people being nit-picky, too many interruptions, a bad lunch that costs too much, pushy crowds, an unkind comment, inability to get through to the right person to clear things, all this can have you figuratively climbing the wall.

You pay a steep price for being pessimistic. Tomorrow won't be better. The boss won't be more pleasant. The work won't flow more easily. Somebody will beat you out on the next promotion. The pay raise won't come through. You read the newspapers and watch the news on TV, and again the whole world is coming unglued. Things happen at home that bug you. Who can blame you for feeling low?

You can blame you, because you're taking it lying down. Who promised you a rose garden? Who told you it would all be easy? Name one person who really had it easy, go on.

Say this to yourself every day as you get up or when you are on your way to work: "A new day, a new chance to do something for myself, a new chance to find better ways to live my life."

Try it. It'll work for you. Optimism is a terrific power waiting for you to use it— *for you.*

Your own discipline— the magic ingredient

We don't like the word "discipline" in this country. It has come to have the connotation that other people discipline us. Parents discipline their children. Teachers discipline their students. "Discipline" has come more to mean punishment than development by exercising self-control.

You are using *some* discipline every day in relation to your job. You arrive at work on time, you do what you feel you can handle, and you take an interest in achieving results from that work.

But are you really working at disciplining yourself for bigger things in the business world? You can develop yourself every day by exerting self-control aimed at doing your job a bit better today than you did it yesterday.

There is a deep satisfaction in doing our job well. But there is no satisfaction in coasting along, waiting for things to improve. You are the one who will make things improve. No one else can do it for you.

Here is how you can start your own discipline program to further develop yourself so that you'll be more prominent in achievement and more visible for promotions, pay raises, and executive appreciation:

1. At the start of each day make a list of the "Things that must be done." Give them a priority—1, 2, 3, and so on.

2. Start on No. 1. Get it done. Start on No. 2. Get it done. Start on No. 3, and get it done. Keep at it.

3. Make a list of "Things I should do today." If you get your

priority tasks out of the way, start in on this list. Check the items off as you get them accomplished.

4. Cut down on distractions. When you have to, cut out the coffee break, take a shorter lunch hour, stay a few minutes after work. Single-mindedness is terrific in getting things done, but distractions will get you off balance. Have someone take your calls for an hour or so if you feel it is necessary. Close the office door. Concentrate on doing what must be done.

5. Foil yourself. All of us have habits that disorient us. If we feel we're working too hard, we begin to feel sorry for ourselves and look for a way out, a way to goof off. Fight this tendency. Stick with the job.

Self-discipline is vastly difficult. You can't hold it for long periods of time; but when you can hold it, you can make your discipline work wonders. The idea is not to "look busy" doing little things but to "be busy" doing the important things. Your sense of rightness tells you when you're doing either one.

Why discipline yourself? The answer is simple. You won't ever be as effective on your job being undisciplined as you will be when you are self-disciplined. Being effective means you're being a success.

Why be a washout when you can be a success by disciplining yourself?

Do you shake when giving a talk?

Everyone gets a little nervous when they have to get up in front of a group and give a speech or a short talk. Even the person who exhibits the smoothest appearance has some tightness inside. It's very normal to have some anxiety about being accepted when one gets up in front of other people to speak. Actors and actresses are often plagued before opening night when a new play is to be presented.

Businessmen and businesswomen are no exception. Many of

them actually like the opportunity to persuade others of their views, but they pay some sort of price in nervousness. People who speak well have learned to control the butterflies, to more or less make the little devils fly in formation.

Here's what you can do to prepare yourself when you know you will be called on to speak.

1. Remember that the group *wants* to hear what you have to say.

2. The best defense is to be well prepared. Write down your most important points. Rehearse them until you have them well in mind. Say them out loud at home until you feel at ease with them.

3. Use notes and hold them in your hand or have them on the table or lectern before you. It is no disgrace to look at notes.

4. Have good eye contact. Look at people's faces as you talk.

5. Remind yourself not to drone on in a monotone. Talk naturally, a bit more forcefully than in a plain conversation.

6. Use gestures, but keep them natural. After all, you are *performing,* and you must use physical motions as well as your voice to put yourself across. Practice these before a mirror at home.

7. Don't speak too long. Ten minutes is a fine length of time; twenty is acceptable, but after that you begin to lose people's interest and concentration. Brevity is still the soul of intelligent communication.

8. Mark your script where you want to pause, where you want to emphasize a word or a phrase. Underline these key parts so you won't miss them as you go along.

9. Be prepared for questions, and don't take any questions personally. Not everyone understands what you said. Some people will miss your best points. Be patient with questioners and give them full answers. Stay with the specific answer, however, and don't digress into other areas.

Giving a talk isn't all that difficult. *You* make it difficult by making it more anxiety-provoking than it is. Look at each speaking effort as an opportunity to show others that you know what you're talking about.

Giving a good talk is an excellent way of building a respected image of yourself.

What to do when you really hit bottom

You live in a flow of highs and lows. Sometimes you get so low that you're lying flat on the bottom of your emotions. Sometimes things look so bad to you that you are almost tempted to give up and let the damn world get along without you. A long series of unpleasant events will take you down to the bottom of the emotional pit. There are days and weeks when nothing seems to go right and you suffer black thoughts.

It is impossible to escape having minor moods of depression. You read the newspapers and watch the TV news programs, and it is all very depressing. You look at some of the things going on in your company and it is equally depressing. There seem to be trouble, bombing, kidnappings, terror, difficulties, and scandals everywhere. You have plenty of your own problems earning a living.

You feel depressed because you "can't do anything" about the situation. Try these steps to fight off those moods of depression:

1. Reality   There have always been wars, barbarism, deceit, viciousness, greediness, and ugliness in the world. The world isn't about to change overnight. You'll see more of the same. No job is without problems that seem to be without solutions.

2. Logic   You can't do anything to correct a situation that has become a social cancer. Some of the job problems are beyond your control. You *can* do something to correct your attitude that leads you to feeling depressed.

3. Action   Don't brood on the situation. Don't allow yourself to feel helpless, indignant, moody. Turn your attention to something from which you get pleasure—a good TV program, a good movie, a good book, or a spirited conversation with someone in the family. For a while, don't read the newspapers or watch the TV news programs. Why let them push your depression button? Let the job take care of itself for a while. Give yourself a short vacation from the ills of the world and from the job problems.

In short, take the pressure off. Let your natural love of life be restored. Do this as often as you must, in order to keep from feeling depressed. Depression is a robbing emotion. It robs you of your energy, your forward thrust, your enthusiasm for life.

Don't let the world or the job mug you.

What kind of person do you really want to be?

I've asked this question of scores of people, and I'm no longer surprised by their answers. An astonishingly big percentage of them had absolutely no idea of what *kind* of person they really wanted to be. Invariably they would say "rich," "successful," "an executive," or "on top of the heap."

You can see how they confused the question by relating it to *material goals* and not to the *kind* of person, to the *characteristics and inner strengths,* I had in mind. Certainly, a person becomes rich, successful, an executive, and lands on top of the heap by developing the proper characteristics and inner strengths. But their answers still put the cart before the horse. All they saw was the finish line and not how they had to prepare and train themselves for the race.

Let's say I asked the question of *you:* "What kind of person do you really want to be?" Your answer would contain some of these deep insights:

1. I want to be in charge of my life.
2. I want to be respected, admired, and appreciated.

3. I don't want anything handed to me the easy way; I want to earn my way in life and deserve what I can win.

4. I want to be friendly toward all people, to respect them, to be courteous to them.

5. I want to control my natural fears of failure, newness, change, conflict, responsibility, criticism, and strange situations.

6. I want to like and appreciate myself and feel that I am solid, talented, dependable, contributive, and needed.

7. I want to feel that my life has been meaningful, that it has been graced with dignity, compassion, love, gentleness, and understanding.

These characteristics and inner strengths constitute the *kind of person you are already*. It is the *goal* of your life to keep improving them. When you work toward *this goal* consistently and determinedly, you have a splendid opportunity to reach the *other goal* of being rich, successful, an executive, or on top of the heap.

Your vital task of developing contacts

You're not giving yourself a break if you don't build good business contacts *outside* your company. Your job, which seems at the moment to be safe, could abruptly be jeopardized through no fault of your own. A merger, an acquisition, a new management team, or dozens of other unanticipated events can leave you wondering what hit you.

That's one of the realities of the business world. How do you go about protecting yourself? Outside contacts, properly developed, can prove to be a lifesaver.

Take the trade associations connected with your company. They provide a rich source of good contacts for you. A highly rated manager whom I've known for years put it this way: "You meet a lot of people when you attend trade association meetings. These are valuable contacts, particularly if you find you must change jobs. Your association contacts can give you some terrific leads."

The contacts become better if you become involved in the management of the association, serving on committees and holding offices. This exposes you to more of the leaders in the association and boosts your stock with them. They get to know you better, are more capable of judging you, and are more disposed to recommend you for another job somewhere else if you should suddenly need one.

Executives, in particular, and the top- and middle-level managers make just such use of the trade associations. You can do the same. Even if you have to pay for your own membership, the effort and the cost are well worth it. You also learn a lot about your company's competitors, you broaden your business outlook, and you learn a lot which helps you with your job. You can't lose.

Like every endeavor, you get out of an association what you put into it. If you're active in one, you win either way. And it's nice to have these good contacts to fall back on if an emergency arises involving your job.

If you're not now active in a trade association, get started. *It's good job insurance.*

How you can merchandise yourself for a new job

One of the most difficult things for any of us to do is to "sell" ourselves to a new employer. We just can't go in and say, "Here I am. I'm ready to go to work for you." We must *convince* the prospective employer that we're a good bargain.

Say the situation arises where you finally decide, after much soul searching and inner torment, that you want to look around and get a better job. How do you merchandise yourself so that you can score quickly and well? Here are some valuable tips:

1. *Pick a number of companies* You've already been impressed by what you've heard and read about a number of companies. They seem to be places where you'd like to work. Make a list of them, giving them priorities.

2. *Do your homework* Before you contact them for a job, call or write the personnel departments and ask them to send you the company literature, annual reports, and recruitment brochures. Read up on the companies to determine whether they *are* the kind of places where you want to work.

3. *Prepare a realistic résumé* Remember *this* rule: An employer wants to know what you can do to help that company solve some of its problems. An employer is looking for a person with certain skills and experience to fit into a job and help get some of the work done. Emphasize at the beginning of your résumé *exactly* what you can do to help that company. Then *support* this proposition with an effective arrangement of your experience. First your jobs and your responsibilities, then your education, then your outside activities. You're a *salesman* at this point. You're selling what you can do for the new company, based on what you did for the previous companies where you worked.

4. *Check your appearance* When you go in for your interview, dress tastefully. Conduct yourself calmly and with control. Don't over-talk, don't gush about how good you are at your present job. Present everything in the terms of how this experience can be put to good use at the new company.

5. *Ask questions* Your interviewer has talked to a lot of people and knows how much *not* to tell you. She or he isn't going to tell you about all the faults of the new company. Usually the interviewer will stress the *benefits,* such as a pension plan, a profit-sharing plan, insurance, and paid vacations. Your job is to determine as best you can the *facts* about whom you'll be reporting to, what exactly will be expected of you, what the company pay increase policy is, what support you'll be given, and other factors involved with the job. Get it all clear with the interviewer so there will be few misunderstandings.

6. *Case the boss* If you strike a responsive chord with the interviewer, you'll probably have a chance to talk to your prospective boss. This is the person you'll be taking orders from. What's your first impression? Warmth, congeniality, interest in you, easiness? Does this person tell you what will be expected of you, fill you in on the important details? Or is there a coolness, a detached attitude? Do you get the feeling this boss isn't really interested in you? What sort of questions are asked of you? What sort of answers do you get to your questions? Your instincts will serve you well. If you go away with strong doubts, you probably shouldn't take the job. If you feel that this potential boss would treat you *fairly* and that your talents *will* be put to good use, you may have found the right spot. The decision is yours.

7. *Negotiate* Good pay and good working conditions are important to you. If you feel that you're not being offered what you're worth, *negotiate.* Don't be in a rush to take what is offered you if it doesn't meet your requirements. Stick up for yourself and get it all understood, in writing if at all possible.

Merchandising yourself for a new job is a tough assignment. You have to steel yourself for the ordeal. Being prepared, as always, is half the fight. But if you're going to spend a number of years working for *this* company and for *that* boss, your preparations and your negotiation will pay you excellent dividends.

Too many people have grabbed at any job and found themselves in a worse bind than the one they thought they were getting out of. *Don't let this happen to you.*

Using ads and agencies to find a better job

In the previous section, you went job hunting on your own. This is ideally the best way, particularly if some of your good contacts have helped you spot an opening and even put in a plug for you. But say this condition doesn't exist for you, and you are forced to fall back on job advertisements and employment agencies. Here's a handful of tips:

1. *Newspaper ads* Depending on the type of job you're looking for, placing your ad in the Sunday business section of your local newspaper should be considered. Some very successful job hunts have been handled this way. It costs you a fair buck, but it can be worth it. The classified or display advertising department of the paper can give you some assistance.

2. *Help wanted ads* Here the companies are advertising for you. Your résumé is the tool to reach these employers. Some print their names; others use box numbers. If your résumé sparks interest, you'll get a call from the personnel department. Send your résumé in with a short covering note accenting the exact skills you have that you feel they are looking for. If you don't hear, it's because someone else did a better job of merchandising through the résumé technique.

3. *Employment agencies* These range from the superb to the ridiculous. The better ones interview you extensively and then try to place you where your talents can really be put to work. Be wary of the smaller ones. They may try to get you a spot where you don't belong. Don't believe everything an agency tells you. Check things out yourself, and don't be rushed.

Whatever method you use, you're better off if you look for a new job while you still have a job.

Coming face to face with deliberate cruelty

You can go through your entire life without meeting someone who is deliberately cruel to you in the business world. It could be your bad fortune to come face to face with someone who thoroughly enjoys pushing people around. How do you handle it?

You put a stop to it at once.

There is no law in this land that says you must remain in a job and take this sort of thing. The first time you are exposed to this type of stupidity on the part of someone in your group, even if it is a boss, it is your responsibility to produce such an outraged howl directly to this person that it will never happen again.

If the sadist keeps it up, go right to the boss and breathe a little fire in the boss's face. Don't pull your punches. If the sadist *is* your boss, go to the boss's boss and raise the roof an inch or two.

If nothing is done, and the sadist is left untouched, you know the score. That is not the place for you to work. Get out and look for another job. Life is too short for you to accept any form of business world cruelty.

Avoid getting stuck in an ulcer job

Speaking of business world cruelty, as we were in the previous section, one of the most cruel situations existing in the American free enterprise system is the "ulcer job." This is the type of job that is unstructured, ripped by big and little crises, and marked by the jobholder's inability to control the situation. There are a lot of these jobs around.

A large number of people in the business world have ulcers. They may have gotten them from their personal life and not from the job. But many jobs can lead to ulcers because of frustrations, heavy workloads, irresponsible management from above, and a setup situation where the jobholder just can't win. Invariably, an ulcer job is a setup situation stemming from a *boss* who is poorly equipped to supervise others and does it dramatically.

It shouldn't take you long to decide whether *your* job can lead to an ulcer. You suffer emotionally, and this leads to psychosomatic illnesses such as an ulcer, colitis, persistent head-aches, even a heart attack. When this sort of thing begins to grab you, you are being *warned*.

The warning is, get out! If you can't change the situation, you're headed for an unnecessary illness. *You're in charge of your life*. Take charge and move yourself to where there is challenge and opportunity but not at the price of a costly ulcer.

Are you emotionally equipped for leisure?

What do you do when you're not at work? How do you relax? How do you do the things you want to do, the things that you work so hard to get money for? After all, the idea behind work-ing is to get the financing you need to do the things you *want* to do. The trick of spending your free time is to do what pleases you.

There is some confusion about people who are constantly on the go. Some, it is clear, are obsessed with the need to feel they are absolutely essential to the office or the plant. They work late, take work home, or show up at the place on Saturdays. They devote most of their free time to the boss and the job.

Others are just as busy, but they are doing things for them-selves and their families. Americans have an enormous amount of energy. Behind this are the facts that we are better fed than many other nations around the world and have incomparable medical services. We have more cars than any other nation and more roads to get about on. We also have more capital income to spend on movement.

Where do you fit into this picture? Are you obsessed only with success on the job, or do you have a normal desire to live life as fully as you can? The obsession with the job, the intense desire to please the boss, comes from your hidden fear of fail-ure, of your unconscious anxiety about the possibility of losing that job or incurring the boss's dislike.

Your desire to live your own free-time life and to enjoy travel, sports, entertainment, the arts, movies and plays, dining out, being involved in community events, and other pleasant and challenging activities indicates that you are emotionally balanced. The point is, if you're not living life fully, you have no one to blame but yourself.

Get out and touch the universe

The job isn't everything. We've seen men walk on the moon. We've seen them live in space for months at a time. We've sent spacecraft to study the far distances of our planet system. We have, in short, had our eyes dramatically pulled from the ground by the excitement of space exploration.

Have you explored the space immediately around you? Stop thinking about the job for a moment. Have you taken a long walk and seen a sunset that was breathtakingly beautiful? Have you walked along a sandy beach in the summertime and thought about the wedding of land and water? Have you walked in snow and been captivated by the white mantle that transforms the earth into something more beautiful?

If there is one fundamental guiding rule in the business world, it is this: "Work hard at your job, give your boss a day's work for a day's pay, but do something for *yourself* every working day."

What this means is:

1. Don't be a workaholic, who spends all of the day's energies serving only the boss and the company.

2. Do what you're paid to do and do it as well as you can.

3. But save enough time, in the evening, early morning, lunch time, or whenever *to do what you want to do for you.*

4. This could be night school courses in a subject far afield from your job, but a subject which absorbs and delights you.

5. It could be writing poems, painting, art craft of any kind,

writing a novel, coaching a Little League team, making jewelry, working with photography, or planning ahead for your own business venture.

6. In short, don't give your heart and soul to the boss and the company. *Save some time for you.*

This fundamental guiding rule is ignored by many people who believe, wrongly, that there is plenty of time to do things for themselves later on. The trouble is, later on comes much faster than they're prepared for. They are in trouble then because *they didn't plan their lives around what they really wanted.*

You're smarter than that, aren't you?

How all these things help you draw your map

"I can't believe what happened to me," a retired newspaper-man told me at lunch one day. "Everything went so fast. One day I woke up and I was sixty years old." He paused over his coffee. "That was pretty alarming. I told myself I'd better get busy about my dream plan. Then I woke up on another morning and I was *sixty-five* and they were saying goodbye to me!"

My newspaperman friend confessed he hadn't intended to stay on a large Chicago daily. He had always wanted to "get a little bit ahead" and start a small resort complex in upper Wisconsin. The time had never seemed right. Now time had run out. It had flown by.

All of us, *you included,* can't seem to understand the ability of time to fly so fast. None of us can look ahead and see the day when the alarm clock goes off and *we* are sixty-five. It's just as well; who wants to brood excessively on the passing of time?

The point is, *you* have no way of slowing down time. The wise men say, "Each day is lost to eternity. It never returns." Put it this way: *waste a day not doing something for yourself, and you've slipped a day behind.*

Many senior citizens, looking back, express regrets that they didn't do more things they enjoyed, didn't achieve their "dream plan," didn't build for their "old age security," didn't travel more widely, read more extensively, become better educated. Regrets, deep regrets, over "lost time."

Don't allow this to happen to *you*. *Now* is the time to do things for yourself, not at a distant point in the unclear future. *Now* is the time for you, at whatever age you are, to draw your map to find the treasure of success. *Now* is the time for you to *get busy* following that map. *Now, not* tomorrow!

10

Who's the New Boss? Why, It's You!

Why not? Why shouldn't you develop your capabilities to the point where you can become a boss? There's an old saying that you are what you believe yourself to be. If you believe you can be a boss, and work at it, *you can become a boss.*

This chapter examines you as the boss. It will put into perspective for you the things you will face when you are in charge of a group, a department, a division, or another business element. Suddenly, the focus shifts. It is not you looking at the boss. It is the boss looking at the boss!

I'm going to assume that at this point you know your boss's job. You *are* capable of holding it. What forces will affect you that up to now have not been of concern to you? What will change? Will the changes be subtle, almost unnoticed by you? Will the changes be drastic, overpowering?

Surely there will be changes in your outlook. There will be

changes in the way you regard the people under your command. There will be changes in the way they regard you, whether it is your "old" group or a new one.

Being boss means you're earning more of the good things of the business world: money, prestige, power, opportunities, challenges, and benefits. You will also inherit some of the not so pleasant responsibilities for profit, for production, for other people's work.

Let's turn the pages and see what's in store for you, the new boss.

The title sets up your authority

Whatever title you have as a boss clearly defines the authority you have. No matter who has this title, the authority is the same. It has been structured by top management on the organization chart. From the job description, you know clearly what is expected of you. It is the title that counts, not the person holding it.

The people in your group know what is expected of you as well. Your first task as the new boss is to get a firm grip on what you are supposed to be doing. Your next task is to see clearly the goals you are being asked to reach and to develop the strategy of reaching them.

You are on a new level of responsibility. Authority over people can be assumed to a certain extent, because everyone is title-conscious. You will be cloaked with a mantle of leadership created by the title of your position.

As a leader, you will be expected by those above and below you to do the things that fit precisely with the title. Your learning has moved into a new phase. There is much to absorb and much to do. That's why a balanced perspective on being a boss is extremely important to you.

Routes some bosses
follow carefully

Being a boss may look easy from a distance. Any boss will quickly set you straight on this point. Most bosses are very careful in following the route they are expected to take by top management. First, they want to keep their jobs. Second, they want to use their jobs as springboards to better ones.

You should review the routes some bosses follow carefully. Like these:

• Established rules governing authority boundaries which prevent one boss from coming into conflict with another

• The organization chart for your group which has been set up to accomplish the group's major purposes

• The system of delegating authority, work assignments, and priority of activities, predetermined to enable the group to reach its objectives

• The system of reporting upward on accomplishments, problems, emergencies, new development, recommended changes, and the like

• The system of cost accounting, budget control, and profit making

On these factors, and others, bosses are judged by their bosses. Every boss has a boss. You'll be very much aware of *this fact* as a new boss. That's why you'll be careful to follow the established rules.

Why some bosses
defeat themselves

Some people never get the hang of being a boss. They are unable to adjust to the requirements of the title. They want to run the job out of their emotions rather than from their logic and objectivity. Some bosses defeat themselves by:

• Breaking every rule top management has laid down

- Bypassing their own bosses and invading other bosses' territories
- An inability to effectively delegate authority
- Messing up the lines of authority within a group so that no one clearly understands his or her specific functions
- Trying to do everything, being all-important everywhere
- An inability to clamp down and straighten out procrastinators
- Constantly saying something along the lines of "I'm not cut out for this job" and lowering everyone's opinion of them
- Being unable to adjust to change in company direction or new top executives, and turning to "ill health" to escape facing the changes
- Feeling inadequate and building a fence to keep people as far away as possible

Some bosses do defeat themselves. They allow negative or runaway emotions to take them into blind alleys. They find themselves on the outside, sooner or later.

How you, as boss, hold your group together

You quickly come to the point where you realize that the title covers you with authority but the people in your group have miraculous ways of escaping your authority. How do you prevent this? How do you build an enterprising group of people who will make you look good and help you win more promotions?

You have a number of ways to consider:

1. *Getting your people to identify with you* If they feel that you're going places in the organization, they're more likely to support you. Everyone likes to be on a winning team. You must show them you know what you're doing. In a way, it's a form of unfolding entertainment with a bit of excitement in it.

They identify with a mover—more particularly, with a colorful, interesting personality who is a mover.

2. *Spellbind them with "security"* Not as effective as the first, but workable. The central feature is that you can give them pay raises, help them with the profit-sharing fund or pension fund. You help them by keeping them on the job where they can rack up years in these funds. You keep them because they must consider what they'll lose financially if they move to another company.

3. *Hold them with money alone* That's it, just money. They remain with you simply because of their paychecks and for no other clear or common reason. They don't see you as a leader, only as part of the payroll department.

Which of these ways is best for you?

As a boss, what changes will affect you most?

There is something about being placed in charge of other people that emotionally changes everyone involved. For your part, you have the realization that *you are really starting upward*. It is the feeling that you can win some of that gold near the top.

But you note that people tend to move away from you. You're not asked to join your old friends at lunch so often. Your new title is now a barrier; you made it and they didn't. You're working on different levels. They're going in one direction and you're moving in another with new responsibilities and new areas to enter. You begin slowly to make new friends of other people at different levels within the organization.

Things do change. You realize this and you're prepared for it. You slowly let the past loosen its grip on you and allow the present to embrace you. The cold reality of your new responsibilities has its effect on you.

You become highly conscious of your authority. You like

being introduced as the "new boss." You like meeting the higher-ups. You like the excitement of the new job.

If you didn't change, you wouldn't be human.

Can you show them mountains to climb?

You still can't do it all by yourself. You need the people in your group as much as they need you. In addition to getting your people to identify with you, can you show them some mountains to climb? This means you work at transmitting to them, in everything you say and do, that you know where you're going and that the way is exciting.

Who doesn't like the idea of mountains to climb and new valleys to discover? Does this sound corny? You can do it. You can establish such an image of authority that your people feel you really understand them and know them as individuals, that your rapport with them is such that you can take them with you on a highly interesting journey in the business world.

Much of this you do by effective communications to them, one on one. The real basis is your genuine belief in yourself. Remember, we said, "You are what you believe you are" some pages ago? "If you believe, you can achieve" is another way of putting it.

Don't miss this opportunity to build your group into a fine working unit. Show them that you intend to go places, and that with imagination, innovation, dedication, and hard work *all of you can get to where the view is more exciting.*

Do you want a short list of boss rules?

Here is a short checklist of pointers—boss rules—which you can consider now that you're a boss yourself:

1. Good decisions are arrived at by the process of eliminating trivial items and unnecessary facts.

2. You learn by asking questions.

3. Don't do things you're not good at; assign them to experts.

4. Criticize yourself objectively, tough as it is.

5. Spend time thinking things over, meditating in a quiet place.

6. Don't rush into things until you have all of the facts.

7. Don't commit yourself to a course of action unless you are thoroughly convinced it will help you reach a group objective.

8. You, and only you, are responsible for your performance.

9. Don't try to work at top speed all the time; shift and change a bit to get variety and refresh yourself.

10. Delegate authority wisely by spelling out all the limitations of that authority and the results that are desired.

11. Prepare yourself for the demands of the next job to which you have hopes of being promoted.

12. Be friendly and cooperative to everyone who reports to you.

13. Keep track of your group's workload so that the primary objectives are reached.

14. Use boss psychology on your boss, establishing greater mutual interests and harmonious friendship.

15. Prepare someone in your group to eventually take your place when you move up to a new job.

Managing frustration as a boss is difficult

Being a boss doesn't protect you from disappointments, resentment, hurt feelings, moods of depression, and anger. Managing your frustrations is difficult because you can't let off steam in front of people. Sure, some bosses do, but it's not a wise practice.

All of us want to be well accepted by our boss and by the

people we command. We want to do our work properly so that we won't face the disapproval of our boss or our group. We don't like the idea of being criticized for our shortcomings or mistakes.

This desire to be accepted and to do well is so ingrained in all of us that we're just asking for frustrations. Things will go wrong. Errors will be made. Crises will develop. Work won't get done on time. If done on time, it may be done poorly. Too many things may pounce on us at the same time.

Accept frustration as part of being a boss. It won't go away just because you're you. Set out now to discipline yourself to manage frustration. The sooner you get to work on it, the sooner you can bring frustration under control.

The problem of knowing what your people are thinking

Are your people thinking what you think they're thinking? That's a bouncy question, but the answer is simply *no*. You can't tell what people are thinking.

Even when they say, "Here is what I'm thinking," you'll never be able to tell for certain that that is, indeed, what they're thinking. They never will tell you everything they're thinking. They may be saying what they believe you want them to say. Most often they are.

Do you tell everyone what you're thinking? Do you include the emotional overtones, the sexualism, desire, intrigue, hostility, derision, or whatever you're *feeling* at the moment? You obviously don't put into words all of your emotions. You screen your emotions out of your words. You protect yourself from being revealed.

It's the same with the people you manage. Don't worry about it. In a way, you *don't* want to know what people are thinking, fully. Your curiosity will burn you, but you have to accept the words they give you. Some of your people are great actors. They can convince you of many things.

They'll never convince you, as boss, that they've told you everything that they're thinking!

What personal life crises can do to and for you

You're the same person at home as you are on the job, or nearly so. What affects you on your boss job affects your private life. What affects your private life can affect your work. It is essential to your good mental health at home and on the job to know beforehand what crises in your personal life can do to and for you.

Think about possible private-life crises such as these:

1. One of your parents dies.

2. One of your closest friends dies of an incurable disease or is killed in an accident.

3. Your spouse has a medical examination and there is a suspected malignancy.

4. One of your children is in trouble with the police.

5. One of your close relatives appeals to you to cosign a large bank loan.

6. Someone in your family totals your new car.

7. After years of marriage, your spouse informs you there is someone else.

Few people escape crises in their lives. You'll have your share. Unless you are prepared to cope with these disasters, they can disable you as a boss for a period of time. They can disrupt your mental stability—even send you off the deep end.

How can you prepare yourself so that you can cope with such thoroughly unsettling situations? You try these thoughts:

1. Terrible things can happen to you as well as to any other person. Call it fate or whatever, such events can happen at any time and quite often from an unsuspected direction.

2. You have three choices: you can go to pieces and forever bewail your unfair fate, you can suffer its impact and let it leave you crushed and unstable for a long time, or you can bear it with dignity and remind yourself of the other courageous persons you have known who have weathered such wicked storms in their private lives.

3. Of the three, which do you want? To go to pieces and use everyone you meet as a wailing wall? To become an emotional cripple who feels nothing but fathomless pity for herself or himself? Or to emerge from the depths of a temporary depression aware that life indeed is very good and that you have the capacity to withstand the torture of private crises and still work at being a fine person in spite of them?

It is unreal to expect that you can go through life without some searing problems within your family. You will be hurt and you will suffer. It is a measure of your true worth as a boss how well you can return your mental health to normalcy and get on with life.

Should you avoid involvement in your subordinates' lives?

The rule used to be: "A boss never becomes involved in subordinates' lives." It's still a good rule, but the swirling field of human relations is changing it. Now it is difficult *not* to become involved. The people who work for you have many needs, and one of their strongest needs is to get both attention and advice from the boss. That's you.

A manager of a woman's dress shop told me, "My salesclerks come to me for help on many of their personal problems. I used to turn them away by telling them, 'I'm sure you'll work it out.' Now I find myself listening sympathetically to them and trying to find ways to help them out of their difficulties."

Lives are more complicated, and more subordinates do need advice on how to work things out. You have two decisions to make. One, is your subordinate who comes to you with a personal problem willfully trying to involve you in order to gain something from you? Second, if you feel the problem is bona fide and there are no strings tied to it to entrap you, can you do something to help that person?

Some people will try to take advantage of your good nature. You can spot these people after a while and turn them off. Others seriously need your help. They come to you because they trust you and feel that you can help them with counseling.

When you decide it is, truly, a matter of trust, then you should involve yourself to the point of giving the best advice that you can. Today that's becoming more a part of many bosses' lives. Your job is to keep it from consuming too much of your valuable time.

Developing your "boss powers"

You're a business executive. Your task is to survive and grow. How do you develop more "boss powers" to push you up toward greater success? There are these "boss powers" to consider:

1. Remaining flexible enough to learn new ways and methods.

2. Being willing to accept change.

3. Focusing your energies on climbing up to the next management job.

4. Avoiding complacency or settling down to one job.

5. A sense of rightness about people.

6. Remaining unflappable when the heat is on.

7. Doing an effective job of telling your people what's going on and what they must be doing.

8. Allowing your people to share in some of the decision-making processes.

9. Getting feedback from everyone.

10. Setting high standards for yourself and those in your group.

11. Working to develop your people so that they grow with you.

12. Making decisions based on all attainable facts.

13. Carrying your share of the productivity load.

14. Never being insubordinate to your boss.

15. Effectively managing time, money, and materials.

No one said being a boss would be easy, did they?

Why your being nosey enriches your boss job

"One of the major reasons many people are successful as bosses is that they are eternally inquisitive," a psychology professor told me. "Inquisitive people are *involved* because they have a tremendous curiosity about people and life and what goes on in this world."

How about you? Have you developed the "boss habit" of being nosey about the world? If you haven't, it is never too late to start. Here are your tools:

1. *Ask, "Why?"* when you don't understand something.

2. *Ask, "How does it work?"* when confronted with something new.

3. *Go see for yourself* If you've wondered about a vacation spot, a new building, a new entertainment feature, a new restaurant, a recent development in your company, anything that intrigues you, go see for yourself.

4. *Read about it* There are books available on any subject you can think of. Libraries have them free for you. Inexpensive pocketbook editions make them easily available to you whatever your budget.

You won't fill your mind with useless information. You fill your mind with alertness and knowledge. The broader your knowledge about the world and your company and what goes on in them, the more mature and solid you become.

Being nosey builds your storehouse of knowledge. *It builds you as a person and as a boss.*

Working up your program to help your organization

This is where you help pay up for the promotion you got, the one that made you a boss. This is where you pull your weight in helping your organization make profits and reach its major goals. Along with the nitty-gritty work of each day, you must devote some time to assessing just what it is that you can do to help your organization not only to stay in business, but grow, make progress, and do better.

The people in top management aren't magicians. They need help—your help. They can use your fresh ideas. They welcome the thought that you are seriously concerned with the welfare of the organization and are doing some thinking about what you can contribute.

You have a conduit to them: your own boss. Go to your boss whenever you have thoroughly thought out a plan or a proposal. You may meet a wall. Keep trying. Keep thinking about what might be considered in the way of innovative methods, actions, or courses.

First, it gives you experience in "thinking big," and second, some of your ideas might hit home.

As a boss, you'll always be on the go

Today's executives as a group are fantastic movers. Study the crowds at airports. You'll see that a very large percentage of the passengers coming and going are businessmen and business-women. Look at the statistics of private aircraft. Note the large percentage held in corporate names: aircraft used to transport executives here and there. The program listings of business meetings at hotels, motels, recreation resorts, special training areas, and even the nation's universities show how many business people are engaged in travel to attend these meetings.

You and other executives are on the go because business in America is on the go. Air travel has made the difference, along with the superhighways and the ease of automobile travel. Not only are the methods of being "on the go" approved by business, but the *reasons* for being "on the go" are well established.

More than ever there is an increasing tendency for bosses to want to attend business functions "where the action is." Meetings are held everywhere, and often, on subjects of planning, sales, distribution, exhibition, demonstration, problem-solving, finance, government regulations, and whatever.

American executives feel better when they can have quick access to customers, suppliers, plants, associates, trade organizations, and a myriad of other adjuncts of their world. There are executives who boast they travel 150,000 miles a year. That's more than six times around the world. They have airline plaques on their walls to prove it. So will you.

How to strengthen your grip on the success rope

Everyone calls it the "success ladder." Let's you and me call it the "success rope." A ladder implies something inanimate, up which you take yourself a step at a time. A rope implies you can be pulled up, if you're hanging on tightly, and also that you can pull yourself up anytime you wish.

You've made your energy pay off. You're a boss. But there is plenty of success at the other end of the rope you're gripping. Here are some quick pointers to get you thinking about your next successes:

1. *In your present boss job* what are your objectives? Put them down on paper and review them frequently.

2. *For your long-range plan* put down the achievements you really want to score. Where do you want to go in the business world? By the time retirement grabs you, where do you want to be on the long length of "success rope"?

3. *Where up ahead do you need to make friends?* Who are the people above you who can help you move upward? Who are the people who need to know that you're a comer, someone to bet on? Get to know them in a practical, natural manner.

4. *Don't hide your light* You're starting to shine. Let other people above you see your progress. Write an article for a business publication in which you are interested. Circulate copies of it to those who count. Make a speech and tactfully let your superiors know about it.

5. *Be a school kid* You're just starting to learn things, no matter what age you are. Look into the company-sponsored postgraduate MBA plans where you can go to night school for two years. You can take special one-week and one-month courses on individual subjects. Pick up new skills. *There is no substitute for knowledge in the business world.* Take courses that enable you to do a better job. Top management will note this approvingly.

6. *Become involved* Serve on Heart Fund drives or other charitable causes. Be active in your church, your community, and your business associations. Take on just as much as you can properly handle. Become an officer in the civic, social, fraternal, and business groups. You show top management that you have ability outside the office.

These activities strengthen your grip on the "success rope," and you'll find you have been pulling yourself up quite well. You'll find also that another force is pulling you up. That force is top management, encouraging you to climb, climb, climb!

The lesson is that you can't leave your destiny in the business world to luck. You're in charge of it, and the more that you are, the more you'll find yourself moving upward.

Isn't that where you want to go?

Growing bosses are
omnivorous readers

Bobby had been given four minor promotions in three years. His latest one made him the boss of an engineering department of a zippy manufacturing company supplying automotive trim and accessories to Detroit's car makers. He felt he was on his way at last.

His new responsibilities made him suddenly aware of how he had cut himself away from the world during his three-year climb. He'd been so busy absorbing everything about the company and his jobs that he'd gotten out of touch. He made time to go back to an old habit, reading.

His choices were *Business Week, Nation's Business, Forbes, Dun's, Barron's, Fortune, Newsweek, Time,* and *The Wall Street Journal.* Bobby also preferred the *New York Times Magazine* for its definitive articles on a wide range of subjects. He bought books on subjects of interest to him and on his new job.

The world opened up again for Bobby. He once more became aware of the massive scope of American business and of American life. He experienced again the vital sense of being connected to what was going on in the world. He read the local newspapers and trade magazines, paperback fiction, and even the magazines to which his wife subscribed. Not only was his omnivorous reading part of his plan for being a better boss, but he was deliberately preparing himself to move up the ladder to a bigger job.

Carole became head of the marketing department of a large paper products company. She had never lost the habit of intensive reading which she had developed as a child. She read everything she could get her hands on about her industry. Like Bobby, she read the large business publications such as *Business Week* and never missed an issue of *The Wall Street Journal.* She also had a bent for the scientific publications, and, when she could squeeze them in, she read science fiction novels. She was a member of a large book club, routinely ordering the new issues.

Carole and Bobby are examples of the types of bosses who keep themselves abreast of the times by reading at all hours and by reading a wide variety of materials. They keep their awareness of the world around them alive and current. They find that the more they read, the greater their understanding of human relations becomes.

Reading helps keep *you,* as a boss, flexible and alert. The knowledge you absorb from reading makes you a better conversationalist. It helps you make decisions because it gives you a broader base of knowledge to work from. It makes you feel more alive, more on top of things, more associated with your environment.

Where do you find time for all this reading? *You make* time. At the breakfast table, while you commute, at lunch time, instead of watching TV reruns, weekends, whenever. You learn to skim until you find things that really interest you, when you slow down and absorb.

Good bosses are omnivorous readers because extensive reading *helps keep them good bosses.* It helps prepare them for their next step upward. *You* do yourself a huge favor when you read from a wide variety of materials. *Make the time.* It will pay off handsomely for you.

As a boss, you must set aside time to think

How much can you do in a day's time? We've talked about *reading* to improve your perspective of life and the world. We've talked about all of your many responsibilities. As a boss, you'll find that you can't live a calm, peaceful, predictable life. You're *hooked* by a job and a personal life that keeps you on the go constantly with relatively little *time to think.*

Whatever your jam-packed schedule, take some time to do

comtemplative thinking about:

- How well you're coping with changes
- How well you're managing your people
- How well you're meeting your group's objectives
- How well you're planning for events five and ten years from now
- How well you're keeping up with the developments in your company and your industry
- How well you're improving your overall skills as a boss
- How well you're taking care of yourself, getting proper exercise, and watching your diet
- How well you're working with your family
- How well you're controlling your emotions
- How well you're meeting your timetable of success

A quiet period of just *thinking* is essential to your health and well-being. It is essential to your continued growth as a boss. *Make the time.*

How you spot the starters and finishers

You're the boss, and you're studying the people who report to you. Which ones can you depend on to get critical work done? Which ones start things but never seem to finish them? Which ones never seem to start anything but are great at following through?

A starter usually is an innovator, a person who gets a kick out of starting something fresh but loses interest in it after a short time. A starter can be highly creative, putting new touches to old methods. A starter can be a sort of enthusiastic dreamer, a bit more sensitive than the others and sometimes very imaginative.

A finisher isn't so imaginative, nor is this person very creative or introspective. A finisher is more of a follower, going along with the daily work without exhibiting much enthusiasm or coming up with bright, original ideas. A finisher is a person who takes something that has been started by others and follows through to get the work done.

You need both types, but you must understand the critical roles that people of both types play. Your job as boss is to spot those who will take on a project and get it started. Then decide who will take over the project and get it done. The nice part about being able to spot these people is that they make it easy for you.

The starters will be in to see you frequently with ideas and suggestions. They're eager to get something new on the front burner. They'll be somewhat excited about the prospect of a new adventure. They may even have it all worked out on paper—objectives, techniques, costs, anticipated results. The whole works. Nothing makes them happier than to have you okay the project. Away they go to get it into the mainstream. But as the project gets under way, they begin to fade.

Here is where you need the finishers. The finishers seldom show up in your office with bright new ideas. If they do, their idea most often is related to ideas about finishing something, not getting a new project under way.

Another word about starters and finishers. Starters are more prone to anxieties, and they sometimes operate in an atmosphere of energetic disarray. Finishers are at the other end, unexcited and plodding.

Not everyone in your group fits into these two broad classifications. Some people can both start and finish a project. Some people can be really enthusiastic about a new project and diligently carry the work right through to the end. So you really have three types: the starter, the finisher, and the starter-finisher.

You need them all. Knowing who is who helps you be a better boss and get more work done, on time and in line with your objectives.

By the way, which of the three *are you?*

Which top job are
you aiming at?

Now that you've become a boss, and logically can expect to move upward, which top job do you have in mind for five, ten, or fifteen years from now? That's a tough question. You, like the rest of us working devils, have difficulty probing into the future and seeing things clearly.

A word of caution. You can set your goals high, prepare yourself constantly, take advantage of your best opportunities, and still be beaten out for the top executive job you want. That's because the business world is never a sure thing. What today seems like a certain bet can be changed swiftly by unexpected events tomorrow. It's happened to many women and men.

The way you prepare yourself is to take the advice of a person I know who was defeated in his plan to become an executive vice president of a petroleum company. "I made all the right moves," he told me. "Education, the right line of jobs stretching up to the one I wanted. Then the board of directors decided to diversify. They bought a number of companies. The executive vice president became president of the new group of companies. I thought I had it made. Then I was told that they were changing the requirements for the executive vice president and that I didn't have the broader background they thought the job needed. They brought in somebody from the outside."

It wasn't this man's fault. The game simply had changed and he was caught in the shift. He did get a better job, but not the one he had his heart set on. His advice: "Select several jobs at the top and prepare yourself for all of them. When you confine yourself to just one goal, you increase your chance of being frustrated. Go for a number of the bigger jobs. That way, you broaden your chance of getting something you really want."

Broadening yourself in this manner is difficult. It means a lot of work on your part. But as long as you know that there isn't a "sure thing" in the business world, you have an excellent chance to make it to one of your choices. Resist the temptation to play it safe and to try to outlive whoever has the top job you want. When you're "next in line," this temptation is great. Go for the broader end of it and make certain the powers that be know you're preparing yourself for several of the bigger spots.

Don't lose your optimism. It may be that in your case things will *not* change abruptly at the last moment and your prize pulled from your grasp. You may have a "sure thing" after all. Who knows?

Charting your financial growth as a new boss

Now you're starting to get more of the money that you wanted. What are you going to do with it? I can't tell you *how* you should put your hard-earned money to work for you, but I will presume to tell you *why* you should start planning a financial program for the future.

Too many young people live from paycheck to paycheck. So do too many middle-aged people. We're a credit card nation hipped on installment plan purchases, overbuying, over-spending, anxious to get expensive homes, cars, clothes, and other material things. We're an impatient nation. We want things now.

One of the best pieces of advice I ever received was never to buy anything unless I had the money to pay for it. In the early years I had to go the installment payment route. I was appalled at what I paid on carrying charges. Credit helps us all get things we need, but we nevertheless must pay for that credit service. My point is that easy credit can lead us into unwise buying and load us with long-term expenses which we could avoid if we'd stick to the cash purchase principle of: "Don't buy unless you really need it, and pay cash when you buy."

What you do with your money is your business. A wise boss,

growing into bigger and better-paying jobs, will sit down and plan an investment program for the future. Your thinking can include buying your company's stock, bank certificates, United States savings bonds, or whatever. You also have your company's pension plan or profit-sharing plan and other benefits. It is wise to always have a cash balance in your savings account at the bank equal to at least three months of your salary.

You might seek the advice of your company's treasurer about investments. You may have friends who are very knowledgeable about the financial field—banking, insurance, and the like. It's always a good idea to have some experts give you suggestions tailored to your income and expectations.

However you go about it, start now to plan your financial program. It is a method of protecting yourself and your family in the years ahead. Don't feel that you have plenty of time. You don't. Now is when you get busy salting some of your earnings away and letting your money work for you.

Your days of pressure, your nights of tension

You pay a price for being ambitious in the business world. You have days of pressure, which is what you're getting paid for. You *can* have restless nights because you bring home the day's share of tension—and you don't get paid for that.

Working for a living can be fun when things go your way. It can be fun when you score the achievements you want, when you make progress, when you're promoted within your capabilities, and when you're treated fairly. You're wise enough to know that the fun can go out of a job because things go wrong or because a big change comes along unexpectedly.

You simply can't control everything over the long haul. Something is always getting out of hand. That's the nature of the business world. A person you've trusted can turn on you. A project that got off to a beautiful start can suddenly fall apart.

Your boss, on whom you've depended, can be out of the picture tomorrow. You name it, it can happen.

Remember the old story about the English king who had a series of disasters? He was hiding, in a cave I believe, after his latest battle in which his army had been shattered. Utterly depressed, he watched a spider trying to spin a web.

Six times the spider tried and failed. On the seventh try, success. The king had failed six times, and the analogy wasn't lost on him. He found the courage to reunite his army, and the seventh time he was victorious.

Now, old stories and fables have points to them. The point here is *persistence*. Surely you're not going to win every time. No one ever does. It's an illusion that highly successful men and women just breezed through life on their way to imminent success. Read the stories of their lives, and you'll find they lost many more times than they won, *but they persisted*.

When you're home at night, after a bruising day of pressure, find ways to relieve the tension. Remind yourself that you are characteristically persistent. You have goals in life. You have talent and skills. You have won some success. You're on your way to more success.

Remind yourself how few sports teams won *all* their games, how few politicians won *all* their elections, how few movie stars had *all* their films nominated for Oscars, and how few of your friends have won *all* their goals in the buisness world.

In short, try not to take the business world so personally. It's not out to defeat you—to create problems and tension for you alone. As a growing boss, you're just being exposed to more frustrations and stress situations, which lead to restless nights *if you let them*.

Try to take your mind off what's bothering you. A good night's sleep is the best smoother in the world. It smoothes you out for the next day ahead, when you can *persistently* begin again to work toward your goals in life.

Your real life is outside the office

That's right. Being a boss is only part of your life. Your real life is what you do on your own time. Now that you've gotten a fine start on being successful in the business world, take note of these cautions about success and its entrapments:

1. If you concentrate only on what happens in the office, you'll end up a very shallow person.

2. You need to maintain strong outside interests, not only in your family but in the areas of social groups, sports, entertainment, and cultural organizations.

3. You can't afford to be caught up in the "win everything" craze in business where you spend every hour of the day working to win more promotions and beat out someone else.

4. You can't, in the same vein, afford to become vain and pompous about your position as a boss.

5. In effect, you can't trade your soul for a title at the office.

The essence of these cautions is to remind you that you are, first of all, an individual who is working to win some significant measure of success from the business world. If you're caught up solely in the chase for success, you lose much of your stature as a human being and become a greedy creature who is self-important to the point of being repulsive.

Balance, that's the answer. Work hard, dedicate yourself; but don't relinquish your rights to stay human, to love others, to enjoy life. But why am I telling *you* this? As a new boss, you have already seen the correct route to go. You'll be a success.

I have confidence in you!

Index